HOMELAND

SECURITY

VERSUS

CONSTITUTIONAL

RIGHTS

HOMELAND SECURITY VERSUS CONSTITUTIONAL RIGHTS

TED GOTTFRIED

TWENTY-FIRST CENTURY BOOKS ■ BROOKFIELD, CONNECTICUT

In memory of the heroes
of the New York City Fire Department
who gave their lives in an effort to save others
on September 11, 2001

Photographs courtesy of AP/Wide World Photos: pp. 8, 11, 17, 39, 47, 76, 89; Getty Images: pp. 14 (© James Virdrine), 15, 68 (© John Chiasson), 93 (© Gabriel Mistral); Corbis: pp. 31 (© Reuters NewMedia, Inc.), 50 (© Reuters NewMedia, Inc.), 58, 63 (© Museum of History & Industry), 81 (© AFP); Roger Jensen/The Oregonian: p. 44; U.S. Air Force: p. 98

Library of Congress Cataloging-in-Publication Data
Gottfried, Ted.
Homeland security vs. constitutional rights / Ted Gottfried.
p. cm.
Summary: Examines both sides of the question: Are we defending our nation against terrorism at the expense of the rights of the individual citizen?
Includes bibliographical references and index.
ISBN 0-7613-2862-9 (lib. bdg.)
1. Terrorism—United States—Prevention—Juvenile literature. 2. Civil defense—United States—Juvenile literature. 3. National security—United States—Juvenile literature. 4. Civil rights—United States—Juvenile litera-ture. [1. Terrorism—Prevention. 2. Civil defense. 3. National security. 4. Civil rights.] I. Title: Homeland security versus constitutional rights. II. Title.
HV6432 .G67 2003   363.3'2'0973—dc21   2003000590

Published by Twenty-First Century Books,
A Division of The Millbrook Press, Inc.
2 Old New Milford Road
Brookfield, Connecticut 06804
www.millbrookpress.com

Printed in the United States of America
5 4 3 2 1

ACHNOWLEDGMENTS

I am grateful to personnel of the New York Central Research Library, the Mid-Manhattan Library, and the Queensboro Public Library for aid in gathering material for this book. Also, gratitude is due my wife, Harriet, for her comments and advice on this text. While her participation in the writing of this series was invaluable, any shortcomings are mine alone.

CONTENTS

Addressing the nation on September 11, 2001, in the wake of the terrorist attacks on the World Trade Center and the Pentagon, President Bush said, "Freedom itself has been attacked this morning by a faceless coward."

CHAPTER ONE

RESPONSE TO TERRORISM

Today, our fellow citizens, our way of life, our very freedom came under attack in a series of deliberate and deadly terrorist acts. The victims were in airplanes, or in their offices; secretaries, businessmen and women, military and federal workers; moms and dads, friends and neighbors. Thousands of lives were suddenly ended by evil, despicable acts of terror.

President George W. Bush on September 11, 2001

On September 11, 2001, the most devastating terror attack in the history of the United States took place. At 8:45 A.M. Eastern Daylight Time, a jet passenger plane crashed into the north tower of the World Trade Center in New York City. At that moment Virginia DiChiara was entering an elevator on the seventy-eighth floor. The lights went out. People began screaming. DiChiara was caught in a shower of blue flame. Alive, but badly burned, she scrambled from the elevator. With help from a co-worker, she managed to walk seventy-eight floors to the ground level. In critical condition, with burns over 30 percent of her body, she was rushed to the burn unit of a local hospital. She was one of those who survived. Many did not.

■■■■■■■■■■■■■■■■■■ THE ATTACKS CONTINUE

Eddie Saiya was a communications engineer who worked on the 110th floor of 2 World Trade Center. He was forty-nine years old with two children—Katherine, sixteen, and Shawn, eleven. "He called me that morning from the roof, calm as could be, and told me to turn on the TV," Saiya's brother Frank recalled. "The first building had been hit. He thought it was an accident."[1] Eddie Saiya was on the roof eight minutes after the first collision, when another jetliner crashed into the World Trade Center's south tower.

Deputy Fire Commissioner Bill Feehan, age seventy-one, was at the World Trade Center when the second plane hit. He organized the rescue effort and called in reinforcements as the chaos increased around him. At 10:05 A.M., the south tower of the World Trade Center crashed to the ground. Feehan and his fellow firemen fled to an underground garage. Here they regrouped and Feehan led them back out to rescue those trapped in the rubble. Feehan was trying to pull a woman out from under a pile of concrete at 10:28 when the north tower fell. He was killed. Deputy Commissioner Feehan was one of 343 firemen who died trying to save others at the World Trade Center that day.

Forty-five minutes earlier, at 9:43 A.M., a third plane had crashed into the Pentagon in Washington, D.C. Just before the third crash, President Bush announced from Sarasota, Florida, that the country was suffering "an apparent terrorist attack."[2] Even as he spoke, a portion of the Pentagon was collapsing.

■■■■■■■■■■■■■■■■■■■■ TERROR IN THE SKIES

By this time there was havoc aboard United Airlines Flight 93 in the skies over Pennsylvania. The jetliner had taken off from Newark International Airport at 8:42 A.M., three minutes before the first plane crashed into the World Trade Center. In

The valiant efforts of New York's police and fire departments saved lives, but the brave workers could only watch in horror as the twin towers of the World Trade Center, symbols of American capitalism, collapsed into heaps of rubble.

addition to the crew, there were thirty-seven passengers on board—four of them hijackers.

About 9:30 A.M. the hijackers killed the pilot and copilot of Flight 93. Subsequently, many of the passengers managed to use their cell phones to alert people on the ground about what was going on. Thirty-eight-year-old Tom Burnett called his wife, Deena, and told her that the plane was being hijacked. She called the FBI. Tom called back and told her the hijackers had killed a man. In subsequent calls he told her, "We're going to do something."[3] Deena told him she loved him. That was the last call.

Meanwhile Sandra Bradshaw, a flight attendant, had called her husband and said that she was going to throw boiling water on their captors while some passengers rushed them. At 9:54 radar revealed that Flight 93 was flying erratically. Fred Fiumano, who received a cell phone call from Marion Britton heard crying, yelling, and screaming. Then the phone went dead. At 10:03, Flight 93 crashed 80 miles (129 kilometers) southeast of Pittsburgh. There were no survivors.

■■■■■■■■■■■■■■■■■■■■■■■■■■ **THE TOLL**

The first estimates of the loss of life following the September 11 attacks ranged as high as 6,500 people killed. Presumed dead as of November 3, 2002, were 3,038. These included the fatalities at the World Trade Center, the Pentagon, and those on the airplanes. The count did not include the 19 hijackers.

■■■■■■■■■■■■■■■■■■■■■■■■ **THE RESPONSE**

While the orchestrated terrorist attack was occurring, firefighters, ambulances, and police were dispatched to the scene from all over New York City. Federal, state, and local officials began taking measures to safeguard the nation from possible additional attacks. All bridges and tunnels in and out of New York were closed. The entire downtown west side of New York City was evacuated, and the United Nations was closed. The New York City primary elections already taking place on September 11 were canceled.

In Washington the World Bank and all federal buildings were emptied. Armed Secret Service agents were deployed around the White House. Both Los Angeles International Airport and San Francisco International Airport were shut down. Flights at all U.S. airports were halted. Trans-Atlantic flights on their way to the United States were diverted to Canada. The Immigration and Naturalization Service (INS) announced the highest state of alert on both the Canadian and Mexican borders. The Pentagon dispatched five warships and two aircraft carriers to protect the New York coast from further attack. The Centers for Disease Control and Prevention (CDC) in Atlanta, Georgia, put emergency response teams on alert. President Bush promised the nation that "the United States will hunt down and punish those responsible for these cowardly acts."[4]

Immediately following the attack, some four thousand special operatives from a variety of government agencies began investigating to determine who was responsible. By September 14 they had compiled compelling evidence pointing to Osama bin Laden and his al Qaeda terrorist organization. Ten days later President Bush signed an executive order freezing bin Laden's and al Qaeda's assets in the United States. Cutting off their money would severely hamper their terrorist operations. "Today," Bush announced, "we have launched a strike on the financial foundation of the global terror network."[5]

It was no secret that bin Laden and al Qaeda were operating out of Afghanistan. President Bush issued a warning to

This launch of an E-2C Hawkeye from the U.S.S. George Washington took place near the New York City harbor. The aircraft carrier provided air defense for the city immediately following the September 11 attacks.

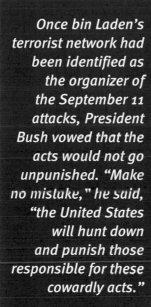

Once bin Laden's terrorist network had been identified as the organizer of the September 11 attacks, President Bush vowed that the acts would not go unpunished. "Make no mistake," he said, "the United States will hunt down and punish those responsible for these cowardly acts."

the Taliban rulers of Afghanistan: They must close the al Qaeda terrorist training camps, turn over Osama bin Laden and other al Qaeda leaders to U.S. authorities, and release all foreign nationals, including Americans, being held by the Taliban in Afghanistan for preaching Christianity. The Taliban refused to meet these demands. On October 7, President Bush told the nation that "U.S. forces have begun strikes on terrorist camps of al Qaeda and the military installations of the Taliban regime in Afghanistan."[6]

The first strike was the carpet bombing by U.S. planes of strategic Taliban sites in Afghanistan on October 7, 2001. On October 19 more than one hundred commandos were parachuted into Afghanistan to begin ground assaults against the Taliban. Over the next month other U.S. special forces units worked with Afghanistan's Northern Alliance, a group that had been fighting the Taliban, to capture Taliban strongholds. On November 25, hundreds of marines landed in Afghanistan—the first major incursion of U.S. ground troops in that country. Other U.S. troops followed, but for security reasons the exact number of American fighting forces involved has not been released by the Defense Department.

■■■■■■■■ THE OFFICE OF HOMELAND SECURITY

The September 11 attacks had badly shaken Americans. Although terrorists had attacked Americans and even the World Trade Center before, nothing of this magnitude had ever happened on American soil via an attack by a foreign enemy. We were no longer invulnerable. Our enemies, it seemed, could strike where and when they chose. It was imperative that something be done by the government to show that action was being taken to protect our nation. President Bush recognized this.

One day after the initial air strikes over Afghanistan, the president issued an executive order establishing the Office of Homeland Security to be headed by Thomas J. Ridge, former governor of Pennsylvania. The order also established a Homeland Security Council to advise and assist the president. The council would consist of the vice president, Governor Ridge, various cabinet members, the directors of the FBI (Federal Bureau of Investigation), the CIA (Central Intelligence Agency), the INS, and others.

Some of the duties of the Office of Homeland Security were:

- Developing, coordinating, and implementing a nationwide strategy to detect, prepare for, prevent, and respond to terrorist attacks within the United States;

On October 2, 2001, Associate Justice of the Supreme Court Clarence Thomas swears in former Pennsylvania governor Tom Ridge to head the newly created Office of Homeland Security.

- Collecting and analyzing information relating to terrorist threats;
- Improving monitoring procedures for early detection of biological, chemical, and nuclear aggression;
- Strengthening airport security;
- Monitoring immigration procedures, visa data, and cargo imports;
- Tightening the security of U.S. borders, preventing entry of terrorists into the United States, and taking steps to deport potential terrorists already here;
- Protecting essential parts of the U.S. infrastructure, such as telecommunications systems, transportation networks, and reservoirs against terrorist attacks;
- Coordinating security for special events such as the Super Bowl, the World Trade Council convention, and the Olympic Games;
- Ensuring that information relating to homeland security was shared among concerned government departments and police agencies at federal, state, and local levels.

To accomplish these objectives, Governor Ridge said that new laws might have to be enacted to give government agencies and officials a freer hand in investigating the September 11 attack and to prevent future ones. Some relevant laws already existed on September 11. Others would be enacted in the weeks following the suicide attacks.

On June 6, 2002, President Bush announced his intention to ask Congress to authorize the creation of a cabinet-level post to take charge of homeland security. In July the House of Representatives passed a White House–backed bill to create a cabinet-level Department of Homeland Security that would oversee twenty-two government agencies including the Coast Guard, Customs Service, and Border Patrol. It would have an annual budget of $37.4 billion and 170,000 employees. However, the bill ran into opposition in the Democrat-controlled Senate where the main sticking point was a provision in the bill giving the president authority to hire and fire workers in the new department peremptorily. Opponents, such as Senator Robert Byrd of West Virginia, say that provision would undercut protections enjoyed by other federal employees and weaken the civil service system.

Osama bin Laden's ties to Afghanistan and the Taliban and his hatred of the United States have a long history. On December 29, 1979, an army of the Soviet Union invaded Afghanistan to shore up the nation's pro-Soviet government that was being challenged by Islamic fundamentalists. President Jimmy Carter of the United States protested and supplied arms to the Afghans fighting the Soviets. These Afghan forces, made up mainly of Muslim fundamentalists, were called *mujahideen*. They included a tight-knit group of Afghans trained in Pakistani religious schools known as the Taliban. Islamic fundamentalists from numerous nations flocked to Afghanistan's aid, including Osama bin Laden. Bin Laden, born in Saudi Arabia in 1957, was the seventeenth of fifty-two children of a rich developer from Yemen. In Afghanistan, bin Laden set up training camps for mujahideen rebels. In 1988 he founded al Qaeda, which originally fought the Soviets in the war in Afghanistan.

In time the Afghans were able to defeat the Soviets. Following the gradual withdrawal of Soviet troops during the late 1980s, conflicts broke out among Afghan warlords and ethnic groups. During this time the Taliban consolidated its power, and, in 1996, it captured Kabul, the capital of Afghanistan. With 90 percent of the country under its control, the Taliban set up a national government to be ruled by Islamic law. To the people of Afghanistan, Taliban rule seemed a welcome alternative to the killing, looting, and crime they had known. But order came at a tremendous price.

The Taliban rule was harsh. Following a strict interpretation of the Islamic religion, the Taliban banned music, television, and movies. The limbs of thieves were amputated. Nonviolent crimes, including adultery by women, were punished by death. Women were forbidden to work or to attend school or to drive cars. They were beaten for not completely covering their faces and bodies.

Meanwhile, bin Laden returned to Saudi Arabia to work in the family construction business, but he was expelled in 1990 for protesting the presence of U.S. troops there. He was adamantly opposed to the Persian Gulf War and the U.S. presence in Saudi Arabia. He took refuge in Sudan where he continued training new members for al Qaeda. In 1993 he was linked to the first bombing of the World Trade Center in New York City. That same year he boasted that al Qaeda had been involved in killing eighteen American servicemen in Somalia. When pressure by the United States resulted in al Qaeda being expelled from Sudan, bin Laden returned to Afghanistan and declared a holy war against America.

In 1998, following the bombing of U.S. embassies in Kenya and Tanzania, which killed 224 people, bin Laden was indicted in a U.S. court for masterminding the attack. Soon after the September 11 strike, the United States determined that bin Laden was responsible and demanded that the Taliban turn him and his terrorist followers over to the United States for prosecution. However, following massive air raids directed at his hidden bunker-type headquarters in the Afghanistan mountains, bin Laden disappeared. His current whereabouts are unknown.

CHAPTER TWO

DEALING WITH TERRORISM

> We're dealing with terrorists who operate by highly sophisticated methods and technologies, some of which were not even available when our existing laws were written. . . . We've seen the enemy, and the murder of thousands of innocent, unsuspecting people. They recognize no barrier of morality. They have no conscience. The terrorists cannot be reasoned with.
>
> *President George W. Bush upon signing*
> *H.R. 3162, the USA PATRIOT Act of 2001*

Prior to September 11 the basic federal law dealing with terrorism was the 1978 "Foreign Intelligence Surveillance Act (FISA)."[1] It was passed following a time of increased terrorist attacks against American citizens around the world and at home. In December 1975 a bomb set off by unknown persons in the main terminal of La Guardia Airport had killed eleven people and wounded eighty others.

Sponsored by Senator Edward Kennedy of Massachusetts, FISA was a product of closed-door negotiations between concerned legislators and the Justice Department. It legalized the creation of a secret panel of judges to hear evidence in cases of wiretap requests or in matters involving secret information that had been classified by the government. Its purpose was to enable federal agents to collect data about suspected spies or international terrorists without revealing their sources or jeopardizing classified information.

During the 1980s a series of anti-American terrorist activities further outraged Americans. On October 7, 1985, members of the Palestine Liberation Organization (PLO) seized the *Achille Lauro* cruise ship and murdered American businessman Leon Klinghoffer. Following this, a bomb exploded in a TWA airliner, killing four Americans, one of them an eight-month-old infant. On April 4, 1986, an explosive device detonated by terrorists at La Belle, a West German discotheque frequented by U.S. military personnel, killed two Americans and a Turkish woman. When the World Trade Center was bombed on February 26, 1993— killing six people, wounding more than a thousand, and causing more than a half billion dollars in damage—there was a public outcry demanding stiff penalties for perpetrators of terrorism.

One result was the passage of the Federal Death Penalty Act, which became law in 1994. It authorized capital punishment for more than sixty federal offenses, including "conspiracy to commit acts of terrorism."[2] The law was strengthened by the Anti-Terrorism and Effective Death Penalty Act passed in 1996. This placed strict limitations on the number of appeals allowed in federal cases involving capital punishment and put a time limit of one year on the filing of such appeals. The 1996 act also authorized seizing the assets of suspected terrorists and of individuals or organizations that supported terrorist groups. Under this law, the presence of a member of an organization at a demonstration supporting terrorist acts is reason enough to seize that person's assets. Demonstrators might also be charged as terrorists and required to prove their innocence.

■■■■■■■■■■■■■■■■■■■ THE USA PATRIOT ACT

Widespread concern around the nation following the September 11 attack demanded the strongest possible measures to safeguard our people and our institutions. While some people were concerned that new laws to counter terrorism might impact individual rights, Congress on the whole reflected the public's concerns and acted quickly to legislate measures to strengthen our defenses against terrorist acts. The result was H.R. 3162, the USA PATRIOT Act of 2001, signed into law by President Bush on October 26.

The new law greatly expanded the powers of FISA. It authorized the FBI to gather domestic intelligence. It enabled the CIA to influence FBI surveillance and to obtain evidence gathered by federal grand juries and FBI criminal wiretaps. The FBI also gained speedy access to medical, financial, mental health, and academic records. The bill strengthened the ability of the Treasury Department to fight money laundering. It authorized the Treasury Department to build up its financial intelligence gathering system and to share its data with the CIA. Prior to H.R. 3162, the agencies were not allowed to share data and had not built up a data bank.

The PATRIOT Act permitted secret wiretaps and secret searches without probable cause of a crime. It allowed government eavesdropping on any telephone a suspected terrorist called as well as on e-mail and Internet communications. The law allowed officials to eavesdrop on confidential conversations between lawyers and clients in federal custody. It broadened the definition of "terrorist activity" to include efforts to raise money for terrorist groups, whether or not the person raising the money knows the group is engaging in terrorism.[3]

The PATRIOT Act also allowed the U.S. attorney general to detain immigrants or other noncitizens for up to seven days without filing charges. After charges were filed, the attorney general could hold aliens for indefinite periods without giving them a hearing or informing them of charges against them, providing he had "reasonable grounds to believe" the person was a threat.[4] Under the PATRIOT Act, any foreigner who endorsed terrorist activity, or belonged to a group that did, could be turned away at the U.S. border or deported.

Concerned about the broad powers being given the federal government under the PATRIOT Act, Democrats and some Republicans in Congress—both in the House and Senate—insisted on a safeguard. This safeguard, called the "Sunset Provision," stipulates that "enhanced surveillance" features of the act would expire unless renewed by Congress in 2005.[5] Attorney General John Ashcroft opposed this provision. He believed that the act should be permanent because it was necessary to prevent further attacks. He pointed out that "it is difficult for a person in jail or under detention to murder innocent people or to aid or abet in terrorism."[6] The Sunset Provision was included in the final bill despite Bush administration opposition, but in a watered-down form that applied only to new wiretap and surveillance powers and not to the entire PATRIOT Act.

On signing the USA PATRIOT Act, President Bush told the American people that "this legislation is essential not only to pursuing and punishing terrorists, but also preventing more atrocities in the hands of the evil ones. This government will enforce this law with all the urgency of a nation at war."[7]

■■■■■■■■■■■■■■■■■ **CONCERNS ARE RAISED**
Not all Americans agreed with this approach. By early December 2001, according to a *Newsweek* poll, "support for giving more power to the government to fight terrorism had

waned since September 11 from 54 percent to 35 percent." *Newsweek* also reported that "some senior officials in the criminal division of the Justice Department as well as at the FBI had also privately expressed concerns about going too far." Specific concerns were addressed by a variety of organizations.[8]

The secrecy provisions set up in the interests of national security drew overlapping protests from journalists and a number of organizations including the People for the American Way, the National Coalition Against Censorship (NCAC), and the Electronic Privacy Information Center. These groups feared that people's rights would be violated behind closed doors.

Some conservatives were concerned that the new powers given to the federal government under the PATRIOT Act would erode the rights of states and communities. The idea of roundups of foreign nationals alarmed the National Organization for Immigrant Rights (a project of the National Lawyers Guild) and the Interfaith Coalition for Immigrant Rights.

Disparate groups, including the National Rifle Association (NRA) and the National Association of Criminal Defense Lawyers (NACDL), opposed provisions that allowed law enforcement agents to use wiretaps for forty-eight hours without first securing a search warrant. *The Washington Post* deplored the relaxed wiretaps and other information-gathering procedures authorized by the USA PATRIOT Act, calling it "a domestic intelligence-gathering system of unprecedented scale and technological prowess."[9]

Some critics worried about provisions in the PATRIOT Act that allowed the sharing of intelligence data among federal agencies and through a nationwide communications system with local police. Critics claimed this practice could blur lines of authority and weaken safeguards limiting agency activities. Prior to September 11 the CIA was limited to espionage activities outside the United States. The new law gave the CIA access to secret grand-jury testimony and the authority to obtain private records seized by the FBI. Kenneth C. Bass, who oversaw foreign intelligence wiretaps at the Justice Department from 1977 to 1981, said that "the zeal, the momentum, needs to be checked and balanced."[10] Most law enforcement officials disagree with Bass, viewing the sharing of information and increased cooperation between agencies as both necessary and logical in the face of terrorist threats.

The American Civil Liberties Union (ACLU) opposed provisions of the USA PATRIOT Act that allowed for "sneak-and-peek" searches by law enforcement agencies. Such searches may be done without the knowledge, or consent, of the person being investigated. The person may never learn about the search at all. Nor would he or she be informed when the agency collected private information, such as credit reports, student records, charitable donations, and banking information. The ACLU pointed out that "prior to the passage of the PATRIOT Act, several privacy statutes required that the government notify Americans when it collected private information."[11]

Following the passage of the PATRIOT Act, but only indirectly in response to it, various journalists and media organizations accused the government of not complying with the Freedom of Information Act. This previous act says that government investigative agencies such as the Justice Department, the FBI, and the CIA must reveal the contents of any files they are holding on a person upon his or her request. Beginning in 2001, these agencies, according to the ACLU, were being told to withhold such information whenever there was a "sound legal basis" for doing so.[12]

Secrecy provisions of the PATRIOT Act caused some people to worry that the government would keep information from the American people. Following September 11, government Web site information was also curtailed. Information about airplane accidents was removed from the Federal Aviation Administration (FAA) Web site. The Environmental Protection Agency (EPA) no longer offered information about accidents and risks involving chemicals over its Web site. Environmentalists and others protested that the public needed this information to protect itself and to demand government action in response to industry neglect.

■■■■■■■■■■■■■■■■■ TRACKING TERRORISTS

In an October 29, 2001, immigration policy directive, President Bush created the Foreign Terrorist Tracking Task Force. The task force was charged with denying entry into the United States of aliens suspected of supporting terrorist activity and of detaining, or deporting, such aliens already in the country. Specifically, it was to deny potential terrorists entry into the country from Canada or Mexico. The task force was to beef up the intelligence capabilities of the INS and the Customs Service and to develop technology to help secure U.S. borders. It was also to institute tighter controls over student visas. One of its goals was to prevent the education and training of foreign nationals who might use the knowledge and skills they acquired to harm the United States.

For some years there had been an influx into the United States of young Arabs traveling on student visas. Some of these visas had expired, and immigration authorities had lost track of many of these young Arabs. The task force was to find these students to make sure they had no ties to terrorist groups, or that they might be involved in future terrorist plots.

There was concern about the privacy and safety of exchange students from Arab countries. Under the federal Family Educational Rights and Privacy Act (FERPA) colleges and universities are barred from releasing students' personal information without their written permission. However, the law allows for exceptions when there is a "safety emergency."[13] Federal investigators used that provision to seek data about foreign students from two hundred educational institutions. Critics charged that "the country may be turning into Fortress America."[14]

■■■■■■■■■■■■■ SECRET MILITARY TRIBUNALS

On October 29, three days after President Bush signed the PATRIOT Act, Homeland Security Director Ridge issued a security alert to the public. He said there was unspecified intelligence information that pointed to the danger of another terrorist attack. It was the second such alert. The first had been released on October 11. A third one, on December 4, warned of "credible" danger of attacks timed to coincide with the end of the Muslim holy month of Ramadan, as well as upcoming Jewish and Christian holy days. Ridge asked Americans to report any "suspicious activity" to authorities.[15] On November 13, President Bush had declared an "extraordinary emergency," and signed an executive order sanctioning trials of suspected terrorists by secret military tribunals, rather than by civilian courts. "It is not practicable," the president said, to try terrorists according to the "principles of law and the rules of evidence" used in U.S. criminal courts.[16]

The military tribunals authorized by President Bush were to have three to seven panelists, all military officers, rather than the twelve member public panels used in civilian courts. Rather than the unanimous vote required to convict in civilian courts, the panels would require a two-thirds vote for conviction in all except death penalty cases where unanimity would be required. The range of possible sentences would include life imprisonment and death. They were considered necessary by the Bush administration in order to try suspected terrorists quickly, efficiently, and without jeopardizing public safety, classified information, or intelligence-gathering methods and operations. The decision was made while an ongoing variety of intelligence information was indicating the probability of another attack. On November 20, the president reiterated his position, stating, "It's our national interests, it's our national security interests that we have a military tribunal available. It is in the interests of the safety of potential jurors that we have a military tribunal."[17]

Authority for the order establishing secret military tribunals stemmed from the president's role as commander in chief. The order would apply only to non-U.S. citizens arrested in the United States or abroad. The president would decide which defendants should be tried by tribunals. The tribunal judges would be appointed by the defense secretary, and he would set the rules and procedures, including the level of proof needed for a conviction. They would admit hearsay evidence banned from traditional courts. There would be no judicial review of tribunal decisions. Defendants would not be ordinary criminals, but terrorists waging war who should therefore be subject to military, not civilian, justice. They were also to protect those involved in a civilian trial open to the public—judges, jurors, attorneys—who might be subject to acts of revenge by terrorists.

In the main, the public accepted this restriction on civil liberties. According to a *Newsweek* poll taken in early December 2001, a month after President Bush authorized military tribunals, 86 percent of Americans believed that the government had "not gone too far in restricting civil liberties

U.S. Attorney General John Ashcroft holds up an al Qaeda training manual as he appears before the Senate Judiciary Committee on December 6, 2001, to explain and defend the need for military tribunals and other legal measures to protect Americans from foreign terrorism.

in its response to terrorism."[18] Yet the call for military tribunals raised concerns from civil liberties groups and others that the rights of individuals might be impaired. Various Muslim-American groups were also worried that members might be singled out for interrogation. A troublesome question was brewing: Could Americans be secured from harm without sacrificing their fundamental freedoms?

Senators also expressed "particular uneasiness across party lines about the rules for the military tribunals that the president decided to create on his own, without Congressional approval or even consultation."[19] They were not alone. William Safire, the conservative columnist, called it an assumption of "dictatorial power."[20] A key question was whether those to be tried before the tribunals were not actually prisoners of war (POWs), and so not subject to such trials under international law. President Bush had authorized the tribunals because the United States was in a war against terrorism. However, Congress had not officially declared war. Did the president have the constitutional right to assume wartime powers? It was not a new question, and President Bush was not the first commander in chief who had to face it in times of national crisis.

■■■■■■■■■■■■■■■■■■■■■ AIRLINE SECURITY
On September 27, 2001, the president announced plans to bolster airline security, including expanding the use of federal marshals—dressed in civilian clothes—on commercial flights. At his behest, on November 16, Congress passed the Airport Security Federalization Act of 2001. It mandated that all airport screening personnel must be federal employees. (The Service Employees International Union, the ACLU, and nine airport screeners filed suit, claiming that the provision was unconstitutional.) The act also ordered that cockpit

doors be fortified and that video monitors be installed to alert pilots to terrorist activity in the passenger cabins.

President Bush opposed allowing airline pilots to carry guns, but on July 10, 2002, the House of Representatives voted to permit them to do so. The government Transportation Security Administration was ordered to train pilots who wished to be armed.

While most Americans agreed that better airline security was needed, some criticized the airlines for abuses. In their effort to screen passengers, airlines resorted to ethnic profiling at many airports, targeting mainly Muslims and people of Arab origin. Indians, Filipinos, and Latinos who had dark skin or wore beards were also caught up in it.

Samar Kaukab, a twenty-two-year-old U.S. citizen of Pakistani descent was one victim of ethnic profiling. Kaukab was wearing the traditional Muslim head covering known as a *hijab* when she was pulled out of a group of airline passengers at Chicago's O'Hare International Airport for a strip search. She was subjected to what the ACLU describes as "repeated and increasingly invasive searches based on her ethnicity and her religion" carried out by a soldier in the Illinois National Guard and three security personnel.[21]

In October 2001, Congressman Darrell Issa, on his way to the Middle East as part of a congressional investigating commission, was prevented from boarding an Air France flight to Paris. Congressman Issa is the grandson of Lebanese immigrants. His experience was one of six hundred cases documented by Arab-American groups between September 11 and the end of the year 2001.

Another involved a Muslim man whose name has been withheld because of the sensitive nature of his government job. He belongs to the U.S. Secret Service and is a member of President George W. Bush's security detail. On December 27,

2001, he had gone through airport security and was seated aboard American Airlines Flight 363 from Baltimore to Dallas when the plane's captain had him taken off the aircraft. Back in the airport, his identity was checked several times by airline personnel and the police. He offered to have the Secret Service confirm his identity, but this was not done. The agent was not allowed to board, and a code was entered into the American Airlines computer system barring him from other flights. When he asked to be allowed to retrieve a jacket he had left on Flight 363, the pilot insisted that "I don't want him back on that plane!"[22]

Incidents involving ethnic profiling were what David Cole, professor of law at Georgetown University, meant when he said that the nation had in effect "decided to trade off the liberty of immigrants—particularly Arabs and Muslims—for the purported security of the majority."[23] Civil libertarians and Muslim organizations agreed.

The Bush administration ultimately called for the implementation of random searches at airports and an end to ethnic profiling. Despite this policy, incidents involving ethnic profiling continued to occur. With the events of September 11 vivid in memory, the airlines and security people had reason to be fearful and wary of further attacks. For example, on December 23, 2001, Richard Reid, a British-born man who became a fundamentalist Muslim, boarded American Airlines Flight 63 from Paris to Miami with explosives in his shoe. He was prevented from lighting them and blowing up the plane by the decisive actions of the crew and passengers.

■■■■■■■■■■■■■■■■■■■■■ ETHNIC PROFILING

Profiling of suspects in America began not with ethnic groups, but with black people. Called *racial profiling*, it describes the practice by police and other law enforcement authorities of stopping and sometimes frisking African Americans on the assumption that blacks are more likely to be transporting drugs than whites. This practice became so frequent on the turnpikes of New Jersey, Pennsylvania, and other states that African Americans ironically dubbed it *DWB*—the crime of *driving while black.*

Similarly, following September 11, *ethnic profiling* became common. There was a realistic fear that Middle Eastern terrorists had infiltrated the country. Authorities reasoned that the only clue they had as to whom the terrorists might be was their ethnic identity. For guidance they turned to the country that had the most experience with fighting terrorists—Israel. One of the first things they learned was that El Al, the Israeli national airline, used ethnic profiling of its passengers and had statistics showing it to be an invaluable weapon in countering terrorism.

Airports and airlines followed El Al's lead and focused on Arab Americans and immigrant Muslims. Most passengers and flight personnel approved procedures that singled out these groups, believing safety took precedence over individual rights.

However, most security personnel at airports and other terminals had no training in ethnic profiling. Hindu women in saris were searched. Men with turbans, prevented from boarding planes, turned out to be Sikhs, not Muslims. Bearded, dark-skinned Latinos were detained.

Such mistakes eventually led to the practice of ethnic profiling being discarded as an official measure against terrorism at most airports. In its place, a random system by which those to be searched are selected by computer was instituted. Believers in ethnic profiling disapproved of the new system, charging that now a wide range of passengers—

from little old ladies to high school girls with backpacks—are needlessly harassed. They claimed that this system doesn't reduce the danger of a potential hijacker boarding a plane. On the other hand, civil rights leaders point out that random searches are more fair and that many innocent people have been spared the humiliation of ethnic profiling.

In any case, the war in Iraq has pushed the issue of profiling into the background. Fear of retaliation for U. S. bombings of Iraqi cities, combined with the hostility of civilian populations towards American tourists in such formerly friendly countries as France, Germany, Spain, and Italy have greatly reduced air travel by U. S. citizens both at home and abroad. Many of the airlines are facing bankruptcy and appealing for government bailouts. They are only one of many segments of the American business community that is hurting because of the combination of September 11 and the Iraqi War. The economy itself has been a major casualty.

CHAPTER THREE
THE DETAINEES

The process of reaching out to foreign nationals and their communities fostered new trust between law enforcement and these communities. The task forces were able to develop sources of information that should give potential terrorists pause.

Attorney General John Ashcroft announces additional interviews of three thousand young Arab nationals

One week after the September 11 attack, twenty-year-old Hasnain Javad was seized by the federal Border Patrol. He was a Pakistani whose student visa had expired. He was taken off a bus and put in a cell with ten other inmates in a county jail in Wiggins, Mississippi. They beat him up. Two of his ribs were fractured and an eardrum was ruptured. His clothes were ripped off, and as the beating continued, they cursed him and called him "bin Laden." Four guards came to the cell and stood outside watching for a while before they reacted to his pleas for help and put a stop to the beatings. They put him in solitary confinement. Javad was eventually released on $5,000 bail. Now he lives in fear that "if I see a police officer, I wonder if he is going to say something to me, question me."[1]

DETENTION
■■■■■■■■■■■■■■■ WITHOUT REPRESENTATION

Prior to September 11, large numbers of young men from Middle Eastern nations were granted visas to enter the United States. Many of these were students who came to attend American colleges and universities. Some came to visit relatives who were either U.S. citizens or resident aliens. Some came to work here, and among those were a few who offered special skills attractive to U.S. firms.

It was true of these Arab and Muslim young men, as it is true of visitors to the United States from other countries, that sometimes their visas ran out, and so they were technically in the country illegally. The procedure for renewing a visa can be confusing and time consuming. Theoretically, any noncitizen whose visa has run out may be deported. Before September 11, it was generally the practice to renew the visa and extend the period the visitor could legally remain in the United States. After September 11, such cases were handled more strictly. Many of these were among those targeted by the Justice Department for interrogation.

■■■■■■■■■■■■■ THE MUSTAFAS/U.S. CITIZENS

Middle Eastern students and other visitors were not the only ones detained by law enforcement agencies. There have been several cases confirmed by the Council on American-Islamic Relations in which Muslim-American citizens have been embarrassed, harassed, and even jailed by federal as well as state and local authorities. Twenty-nine-year-old American-born Nacer Fathi Mustafa was one.

Mustafa was arrested along with his sixty-six-year-old father, Fathi Mustafa, at a Houston airport on September 15, 2001. Father and son were en route back to their hometown of La Belle, Florida, from a business trip to Mexico when

Nacer Mustafa holds a boot from a shipment of 700 pairs at his Merit Market Truck Stop in La Belle, Florida. Mustafa and his father were detained by federal authorities on September 14 at Bush Intercontinental Airport in Houston, accused of altering their passports. Only after incurring $40,000 in legal fees were the Mustafas able to prove that the charge was unfounded and occurred because of the family's ethnic origins.

authorities stopped them and accused them of having altered their passports. Later the government acknowledged that there had been no alteration of the documents, but it did not make clear why it had suspected the two men and why they were being detained.

Nacer was held by the Justice Department in a Texas jail for sixty-seven days. Fathi, a naturalized citizen who has lived in the United States for forty years, was released after eleven days but forced to wear an electronic ankle monitor so that authorities could keep track of his movements. During the more than two months Nacer remained in jail, the Mustafa family accumulated $40,000 in legal fees trying to secure his release.

Father and son believe they were incarcerated only because they are of Middle Eastern ancestry. "I am not the same person I used to be," says Nacer. "I watch the news all the time looking to see if there are more people like me, locked up after September 11 because they have a Middle Eastern name."[2]

■ ■ ■ ■ ■ ■ ■ ■ ■ ■ ■ ■ ■ ■ ■ ■ ■ ROUNDING UP SUSPECTS

Nacer Mustafa's suspicion was justified. In early October 2001, the Justice Department announced its plan "to question five thousand men ages eighteen to thirty-three who arrived in this country over the last two years from nations suspected of links to terrorism."[3] Administration officials from the president on down had made a concerted effort to prevent anti-Arab and anti-Muslim bias. They had reached out to the Arab-American community to support it and to establish ties with it. They clearly wanted to prevent a September 11 backlash similar to the anti-German bigotry of World War I or the anti-Japanese injustices of World War II. At the same time, however, they had to recognize that the thousands of lives lost in the worst terrorist incident in U.S. history had been caused by young Middle Eastern men in this country as visitors. The reality was that among the thousands of innocent Muslim and Arab men visiting the United States, there was a strong possibility that there were those plotting further acts of terrorism. The administration knew that it would be criticized for singling out members of one group for investigation and interrogation, but felt it had no choice: American lives were at stake.

The Justice Department initially targeted five thousand men from countries where terrorists were thought to operate. Prior to the announcement, law enforcement agents from different branches of federal, state, and local governments had already implemented investigations focusing on resident aliens from Muslim and Arab countries. The federal plan encouraged them to coordinate their activities with the Justice Department. It ordered federal agents to work with state and local police to find those wanted for interrogation.

By October 30 some nine hundred of those questioned had either been arrested or had been turned over by the FBI to the United States Immigration and Naturalization Service (INS) and were being held in custody. The Justice Department and the INS refused to release their names, the dates they were detained, or where they were being held. Without this information, lawyers were prevented from consulting with the prisoners. Many of the detainees had originally been picked up for minor traffic violations or because they had been viewed by neighbors as suspicious.

One of these was twenty-one-year-old Salam el-Zaatari. An exchange art student from Lebanon, el-Zaatari was searched at a Pittsburgh airport when he tried to board a plane. An X-acto knife was found in his backpack. Although such tools are commonly used by art students, and other non-Middle Eastern people have not been detained for carrying similar objects, Salam was held in custody for six weeks and not allowed to see a lawyer.

For reasons not disclosed, Osama Awadallah, another detainee, was swept up by FBI agents in the parking lot of his building and subsequently transported to four different jails. He says he was cursed at, threatened by guards, and put in shackles, which cut him. He often went hungry because his religion forbids him to eat much of the food provided by his captors. When he insisted that it was his right to go to prayer service, he was told that "here you don't have rights."[4]

While steps were taken by the government to correct some of the abuses Muslim detainees encountered, federal authorities continued to insist on keeping the identities of prisoners secret. About 150 of those whose names remained unknown were held in the Passaic County jail in New Jersey. Sheriff Jerry Speziale, who runs the jail, stands behind this policy. "A good portion of these detainees are what we call criminal aliens," he insists. "Are these people who came here to Disneyland and decided to stay an extra four days? No."[5] But Sheriff Speziale did not specify why he referred to the detainees as criminals.

■■■■■■■■■■■■■■ CIVIL RIGHTS CONCERNS

Civil liberties groups, Muslim-American organizations, and others protested the treatment of detainees. According to *The New York Times*, members of the judiciary were also concerned. In a September 10, 2002, editorial, the *Times* quoted Federal District Court Judge Gladys Kessler as declaring that secret arrests were "odious to a democratic society." She ordered the government to release the names of all detainees, but the government refused to comply with the order. The *Times* also reported that in presiding over one of the detainee cases Judge Robert Doumar of the Federal District Court in Norfolk, Virginia, instructed federal prosecutors to submit documents so that he could determine if the accused was in fact an enemy combatant. The Justice Department defied his order.[6]

Attorney General John Ashcroft was a focus of concern about excessive zeal when he appeared before the Senate Judiciary Committee in December 2001. Repeatedly asked questions about why the names of people in detention were being withheld, he evaded answering. He also was evasive about why the Justice Department had refused to let the FBI check its records to determine whether any of the detainees had bought guns, while other privacy rights were disregarded. An editorial in *The New York Times* expressed dismay at Ashcroft's change in attitude toward the rights of people under investigation "when the issue turned to the privacy rights of gun owners."[7]

■■■■■■■■■■■■■■■■ REFUSALS TO COOPERATE

Not all local law enforcement agencies were anxious to cooperate with the Justice Department. In Portland, Oregon, assistant police chief Andrew Kirkland was in charge while the chief of police was away. An African American, Kirkland denounced the plan as racial profiling of the sort he had suffered as a black male growing up in Detroit. He was backed up by Portland's assistant city attorney who found that a state law forbid local police to "collect or maintain information about the political, religious or social views, associations or activities of any individual, group, [or] association . . . unless such information directly relates to an investigation of criminal activities, and there are reasonable grounds to suspect the subject of the information is or may be involved in criminal conduct."[8] The opinion was endorsed by the Portland city attorney and the mayor.

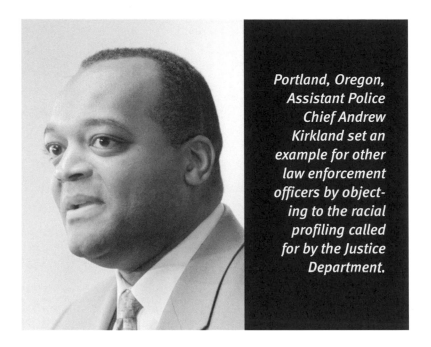

Portland, Oregon, Assistant Police Chief Andrew Kirkland set an example for other law enforcement officers by objecting to the racial profiling called for by the Justice Department.

Other cities followed Portland's lead. Among them were Corvallis—also in Oregon—Seattle, Washington, and the California cities of San Francisco, San Jose, and Fremont. In Fremont, home to the nation's largest Afghan-American community, Police Chief Craig Steckler insisted that "I personally don't think we have any terrorists living in Fremont, nor do I think we have people living in Fremont who know terrorists." Chief Steckler assigned local officers to accompany FBI officers interviewing Fremont residents because "if federal officials aren't respectful, it could jeopardize local relationships." California's San Mateo county sheriff Don Horsley claimed that "we don't have any legal authority to question people. Unless they [federal agents] could articulate some suspicious activity, no, we wouldn't participate."[9]

Lieutenant Horace Frank of the Los Angeles Police Department disagreed. "Nothing that they've asked us to do constitutes a violation of any law," he said. Baltimore detective Gary McLhinney put it more strongly. He recommended that "the leaders of those agencies who decide not to assist should reassess what kind of career path they should take."[10]

■■■■■■■■■■■■■■■■ MORE INTERROGATIONS

On March 20, 2002, the Justice Department announced that three thousand more subjects from the Middle East were to be interviewed. Critics of the program found this puzzling. Investigators had been able to locate only 2,261 people of the original 5,000 targeted for interrogation in the previous October. That was less than half. According to Attorney General Ashcroft, their "best efforts could not overcome the serious flaws in our current ability to locate visitors to our country."[11] Furthermore, Justice Department officials admitted that six months after September 11, the interviews had not resulted in any arrests linked to that attack.

Nevertheless, Ashcroft insisted that the program was worthwhile and that additional interviews were justified. It ensured, he said, that "potential terrorists hiding in our communities knew that law enforcement was on the job in their neighborhoods. Such a climate could cause would-be terrorists to scale back, delay or abandon their plans altogether." He added that the first round of interrogations "may well have contributed to the fact that we have not suffered a substantial terrorist attack since September 11."[12]

While many in Congress, along with many ordinary Americans, agreed with that assessment, others did not. Senate Judiciary Committee chairman Patrick Leahy of Vermont said that the interviews were "a completely useless waste of law enforcement," adding that "I don't think it would accomplish much of anything."[13] Representative John Conyers of Michigan, the ranking Democrat on the House Judiciary Committee, reported that "the national leadership of Arab and Muslim organizations have expressed to me their outrage over this illegal form of racial profiling."[14] Hussein Ibish of the American-Arab Anti-Discrimination Committee was distrustful of "the whole question of investigating thousands of people and compiling dossiers and entering them into a computer."[15]

■■■■■■■■■■■■■■■■■■■■■ **THE IMPRISONED**
More than 1,200 of those investigated were taken into custody. As of mid-March 2002, at least 300 were still being held in detention by the INS according to Amnesty International. Two months earlier, on January 11, 2002, the Justice Department released information on 725 detainees being held at that time. They revealed the detainees' nationality, date of arrest, date that they were charged, and the nature of the charge against them. However, the government did not reveal the names of the detainees nor the locations where they were being held. Nor did the government release information on how many of the detainees had been deported and how many were released back into the U.S. population. This information was still being withheld in January 2003 when six detainees staged a two-week hunger strike to protest conditions at the Passaic County Jail in Paterson, New Jersey. Immigration and Naturalization Service official Kerry Gill said that the agency would consider their demands, but there was no guarantee that they would be met.

Those still being held, according to an Amnesty International report, had undergone treatment forbidden by both the U.S. Constitution and international law. They had

At a January 21, 2002, rally in New York City, Uzma Naheed holds a picture of her husband, Anser Mehmood, who is in the Passaic County jail in New Jersey. Mehmood is one of the many Arab and South Asian immigrants detained since September 11 by the Immigration and Naturalization Service for visa violations.

endured prolonged solitary confinement. Their hands and feet had been shackled while in prison, during interrogation, and whenever they had been taken before immigration judges. They had been denied prompt access to lawyers. They had been allowed phone calls to family only once every thirty days. More seriously, they had been held without being charged for long periods pending security clearance by the FBI. While Amnesty International recognized "the government's obligation to take all necessary measures to protect its citizens from potential security threats," as of the middle of March 2002, the organization was still "concerned that the Immigration Service [was] being used to hold people on flimsy evidence, pending broad criminal probes, without due safeguards."[16]

■■■■■■■■■■■■■■■■■■■ **CORRECTING ABUSES**

Responding to pressure, the federal government acted to correct some of the abuses. In early February 2002, representatives of Amnesty International, the ACLU, and the American Friends Service Committee were granted access to the detainees in county jails in Passaic, Middlesex, and Hudson County, New Jersey, where roughly half of the detainees were being held. They were permitted to inform the prisoners of their rights. The organizations' representatives learned from authorities that some of the prisoners were continuing to be held until the FBI made sure they had no ties to terrorism. Once that determination was made, the FBI said that detainees would either be released or deported back to their native countries.

By early March a coalition of civil liberties organizations was conducting "Know Your Rights" sessions for detainees in New Jersey's county jails. The government cooperated by implementing Immigration and Naturalization Service (INS) Detention Standards that certify that "INS encourages such presentations, which instruct detainees about the immigration system and their rights and options within it." The standards order that "all facilities shall fully cooperate with authorized persons seeking to make such presentations."[17]

The presentations informed the detainees about immigration court procedures, how to arrange for bail bonds, ways to fight deportation, and appeals processes. Prisoners were able to discuss their cases with advisers individually and privately, and translators were provided.

Clearly the government was acting to correct the abuses affecting the detainees. Nevertheless, the prisoners continued to suffer from a lack of representation by experienced immigration lawyers. There is a shortage of such attorneys, and according to J. C. Salyer, an ACLU staff attorney, "It is unreasonable to expect that the immigration court system will produce a fair result when, in so many cases, the government is represented by a prosecutor, but the detainee must stand alone."[18]

■■■■■■■■■■■■■■■ THE TWENTIETH HIJACKER

The most prominent detainee, Zacarias Moussaoui, was not seized in the post-September 11 roundups by the government. The thirty-three-year-old French citizen of Moroccan descent had been arrested a month earlier, on August 16, for a passport violation. Authorities had been called by officials at a Minnesota flight school who became suspicious when he sought training on flight simulators used on Boeing jetliners. They said he had been interested only in learning how to make turns, not takeoffs or landings, and had asked questions about flying in New York City air space. Four months later Moussaoui was charged with having been a co-conspir-

A police photograph shows Zacarias Moussaoui, a French citizen of Moroccan descent, who was charged in connection with the September 11 attacks.

ator of the September 11 terrorists, and of "conspiring with Osama bin Laden and al Qaeda to murder thousands of innocent people."[19]

Government investigators had amassed much detailed information about the plot that resulted in the September 11 hijackings, and prosecutors had linked Moussaoui to it. Like the nineteen hijackers who died, he had trained as a soldier in the al Qaeda terrorist network, had received wire transfers of money from the same source as they did, had bought knives and flight-training manuals similar to theirs, and had first sought crop-dusting training, and then airliner training, which the hijackers had also done. The hard disk on Moussaoui's computer contained instructions on spraying pesticide from a plane. (The government's theory is that there was an alternate plan to September 11 to spread poisoned chemicals or germs.) He had carried the phone number of the terrorists' al Qaeda contact in Dusseldorf, Germany. Fellow inmates said that when Moussaoui heard the news of the collapse of the twin towers, he cheered.

Three of the four planes hijacked each had five terrorists aboard. The fourth plane had only four. The government's theory is that Moussaoui was supposed to be the fifth man, and that only his August 16 arrest prevented him from participating in the attack. Moussaoui initially denied these charges, but prosecutors had compiled considerable evidence linking him to the conspiracy.

■■■■■■■■■■■■■ SEEKING THE DEATH PENALTY

Capital punishment was a possible sentence for four of the six charges of conspiracy that Moussaoui faced. Although the government had never sought the death penalty in a conspiracy case before, on March 28, 2002, the Justice Department announced that it would do so in the Moussaoui case. They acted despite a request to Attorney General Ashcroft by the justice minister of France, Marylise Lebranchu, asking that "capital punishment not be sought against" Moussaoui who was a French citizen.[20] France considers the death penalty to be a violation of human rights.

Ashcroft's response was to ask the international community "to respect our sovereignty" as "we respect theirs."[21] He added that the United States would welcome the cooperation of the French. However, France decided not to cooperate. This denied the prosecution a large file compiled by French intelligence agencies that detailed Moussaoui's ties to al Qaeda.

Organizations that opposed the death penalty protested Ashcroft's response. Some experts in international law also

■■■■■■■■■■■■■■■■■■■■■■■■■■■■■■■■■■

Well before trial, the Moussaoui case raised issues of freedom of the press when *Court TV* and *C-Span* challenged a government ban on TV cameras in federal criminal courts. The networks argued that because there was widespread concern about the trial, there was a constitutional "public interest" in televising it. Defense attorney Edward MacMahon Jr. said that it would provide Moussaoui with "a added layer of protection" for a fair trial. Prosecutors responded that it would jeopardize the security of jurors, witnesses, and court officials. They also objected to providing "the twentieth hijacker" with a worldwide audience for any anti-American diatribes.[22]

Judge Brinkema upheld the ban, declaring that it "does not violate the constitutional rights of either the public or the broadcast media." Agreeing with the prosecution's reasoning, she added that any benefits of televising the trial were "outweighed by the significant dangers worldwide broadcasting of this trial would pose to the orderly and secure administration of justice."[23]

It was an endorsement of the administration's general position that people's safety is more important than legalisms. The right of the media to cover a story had been found less important than the lives that might be put in jeopardy by such coverage. To the administration, and to many Americans, the judge's decision was a victory for common sense.

■■■■■■■■■■■■■■■■■■■■■■■■■■■■■■■■■

questioned its wisdom. If the United States could try and punish a foreign national under U.S. laws not honored in the accused's native country, they asked, what was to prevent such nations as Iraq or North Korea from inflicting undemocratic trials and harsh punishments on American citizens under their laws?

In seeking the death penalty, Attorney General Ashcroft had cited the events of September 11 and "the impact of the crime on thousands of victims."[24] Soon after the trial was moved to Virginia, prosecutors began interviewing relatives of those killed in the September 11 attack. They were doing this because in the second phase of a case, when sentencing is decided, testimony of the impact of the crime on survivor victims is heard by judge and jury. Barbara Minervino, whose husband was killed in the World Trade Center attack, pointed out that her husband was executed and added that "if it's proven that this man had any knowledge and participated in any way, then I support his execution completely."[25]

■■■■■■■■■■■■■■■■■■■■■■■■ A GUILTY PLEA

The legality under international law of trying Moussaoui as a candidate for the death penalty became less of a consideration than the actual extent of his guilt as the trial moved forward. The proceedings became more and more bizarre as Moussaoui insisted on acting as his own defense attorney and behaved more and more irrationally during court proceedings. Things came to a head on July 18, 2002, when Moussaoui tried to plead guilty to conspiring in the September 11 attacks and acknowledged that he was a member of al Qaeda and loyal to Osama bin Laden. He added that he was not directly involved in the September 11 attack, but that he was pleading guilty to avoid the death penalty.

Moussaoui's behavior—his choice of words, his attitude,

his seeming lack of understanding of the laws under which he was being tried, his rambling, combative, and often confusing statements in court—caused U.S. District Judge Leonie M. Brinkema to reject his guilty plea. She told him she would give him a week to reconsider a decision that could guarantee his execution. Moussaoui returned to court on July 25 and withdrew his guilty plea. As the trial moved forward, questions were raised in the media about his mental stability and capacity to stand trial.

The prosecution was also bedeviled by other considerations. In mid-July 2002, FBI investigators, and some government officials, said publicly that the prosecution put forth no direct evidence that Moussaoui had a role in the September 11 attack. They said that Justice Department prosecutors overreached in charging him as a direct participant in the September 11 conspiracy. Attorney General Ashcroft's prosecutors denied this. They insist that the case against Moussaoui remained strong. On February 13, 2003, however, Judge Brinkema indefinitely postponed the Moussaoui trial. The postponement was requested by the Justice Department in order to appeal Judge Brinkema's ruling allowing Moussaoui defense lawyers to question a captured al Qaeda member. The issue has threatened to halt the civilian trial altogether and transfer the case to a military tribunal. Either way, Moussaoui continues to face the death penalty.

CHAPTER FOUR
PRESIDENTIAL POWER AND THE CONSTITUTION

The Constitution is not a suicide pact.

United States Supreme Court
Justice Robert Jackson, 1949

Aside from the question of whether or not President Bush had acted constitutionally in his response to September 11, he had surely acted decisively. Our nation had come under attack. More than three thousand of our citizens had been murdered. He had been quick to respond to that atrocity. The American people recognized this. By the middle of May 2002, a CBS News Poll reported that 71 percent of them approved "of the way George W. Bush is handling his job as President."[1]

Some of those who were concerned that President Bush had overstepped his authority believed his actions were justified. Norman Ornstein of the American Enterprise Institute was one. "You always have to worry about people who have this kind of power who don't have the restraint," he said. "I worry about that. But," he added, "we have such a different kind of threat on the country as a whole that you have to change the way you look at presidential power."[2]

Indeed, there are many precedents for the exercise of extraordinary powers by presidents throughout American history. All of them raised issues of law and civil rights. All presented the presidents involved with hard choices involving serious consequences. Whatever the criticism leveled against him, the use of power by President George W. Bush in this time of terror follows the tradition of former presidents dealing with difficult times.

John Adams, among others, had justified imposing unconstitutional measures for the good of the nation. President George W. Bush and his administration would make similar claims. In citing historical precedents, they would find compelling examples in the policies of presidents Franklin Roosevelt, Harry Truman, and Abraham Lincoln.

■■■■■■■■■■■■■ THE ALIEN AND SEDITION ACTS

In 1798 the nation's second president, John Adams, signed into law the Alien and Sedition Acts. These acts made it a crime to speak or write critically of the president, a clear violation of the First Amendment guarantees of freedom of speech and the press. They "gave the President the power to imprison or deport aliens" without giving them a trial.[3]

Adams's justification for these measures was the recent French Revolution, which he opposed, and the number of noncitizens in the United States who supported it. Adams said the alien supporters in the United States threatened violence. His opponents claimed that the new laws were "designed to destroy Thomas Jefferson's Republican Party," which was sympathetic to the Revolution.[4] Twenty-five people, "practically all of them Republican editors, were haled before federal courts, jailed, and fined."[5]

James Madison called the Alien and Sedition Acts "a monster that must forever disgrace its parents."[6] Thomas

Jefferson said it was a "libel on legislation."[7] When Jefferson succeeded Adams as president, he allowed the laws to lapse, freed those who had been jailed, and had Congress return the fines the accused had paid.

■■■■■■■■■LINCOLN SUSPENDS HABEAS CORPUS

In 1861, at the beginning of the Civil War, President Lincoln suspended the writ of habeas corpus in Maryland. Habeas corpus is defined by *Webster's Dictionary* as an "order requiring that a prisoner be brought before a court at a stated time and place to decide the legality of his detention or imprisonment; the right of habeas corpus safeguards one against illegal detention or imprisonment."[8] Maryland was a Civil War border state whose population was split between Union and Confederate sympathizers. Among those who favored the South were suspected saboteurs as well as orators and newspaper writers whose words, Lincoln feared, might have incited people to take action against the Union.

Lincoln had based his suspension of habeas corpus on Article I, Section 9 of the Constitution, which reads that habeas corpus "shall not be suspended, unless when in cases of rebellion or invasion the public safety may require it."[9] However, others disagreed. When the first case challenging Lincoln's suspension of habeas corpus was heard by Judge Roger B. Taney, he denied that the president had the right to take the action. Article I, Section 9, Judge Taney pointed out, referred to the powers of Congress, not the president, and therefore only Congress could suspend habeas corpus.

Lincoln refused to obey Judge Taney's decision. His justification was that "some temporary sacrifice of parts of the Constitution" was necessary "in order to maintain the Union and thus preserve the Constitution as a whole."[10] When members of the Maryland state legislature responded

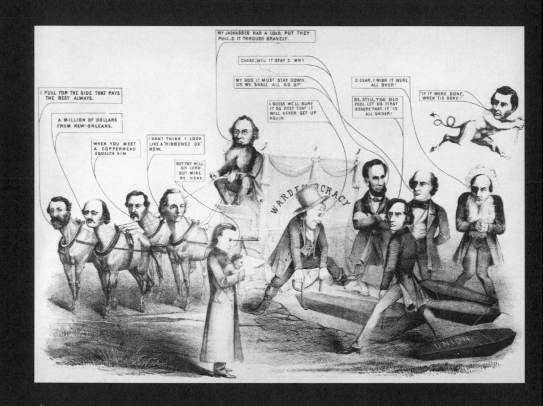

In this 1864 political cartoon entitled "The Grave of the Union," a hearse nicknamed the "War Democracy" is carrying off a number of liberties to be buried, among them Habeas Corpus.

by denouncing the president for "unjust tyrannical acts," Lincoln sent federal troops to arrest thirty-one of them.[11] The Baltimore police chief, four police commissioners, and Mayor George Brown were also seized. The legislators were imprisoned for two months during which time a new legislature was elected. The federal government never offered any evidence that the prisoners were guilty of any crime, and none of them were brought to trial.

■■■■■■■■■■■■■■■■■ **MILITARY TRIBUNALS**

To enforce the exception to habeas corpus, Lincoln had put some of the border states like Missouri and Kentucky, and some sections of the occupied Confederacy, under martial law. Some 13,000 people were held without trial by the Union. Those who were tried—suspected saboteurs, accused spies, recruiters for the Confederate army—were judged by military tribunals rather than by civilian courts. These tribunals also tried Union soldiers who deserted as well as northerners accused of treasonous activity, even though civilian courts were readily available in the states that were loyal to the Union.

One of the Civil War military tribunals condemned four northerners to death for conspiring to overthrow the government. In 1864 one of the four, Lambdin P. Milligan, appealed the verdict and the U.S. Supreme Court set aside the convictions. The Court held that except in war zones, "the substitution of military tribunals for civilian courts is constitutionally permissible only if authorized by Congress."[12] The Court added that even if Congress authorized them, tribunals were not to be used when civilian courts were accessible.

The use of military tribunals goes back to the American Revolution. George Washington used them to deal with deserters, traitors, and British spies. Major John André, the British spy who collaborated with Benedict Arnold, was tried, convicted, and hanged by one of them. In the Mexican War (1846–1848), American soldiers who rioted were tried by a military tribunal. So, too, were Mexican guerrilla fighters, but it was not until the Civil War that military tribunals were used to try civilians.

■■■■■■■■■■■■■■■■■ THE NAZI SABOTEURS

Ex Parte Quirin, a unanimous decision reached by the U.S. Supreme Court in 1942 during the administration of President Franklin Roosevelt, is the precedent most often used by Bush administration spokespersons in support of creating military tribunals. The case involved eight World War II Nazi saboteurs who had entered the country illegally to blow up bridges, defense plants, and other wartime targets. Two of them were American citizens, the other six Germans. They were landed by submarine in two groups, one at Ponte Vedra in Florida, the other on Long Island in New York. One of the Germans, George Dasch, went straight to Washington, D.C., and turned in himself and the others to the FBI.

Soon after the saboteurs were taken into custody, President Roosevelt issued an order closing civilian courts to suspected saboteurs and spies and authorizing a military tribunal to try them. For reasons of national security, the hearings were to be held in secret. A panel of military officers was hastily convened at the Justice Department. U.S. Attorney General Francis Biddle was the chief prosecutor. The constitutionality of the proceedings was immediately challenged by defense attorney Kenneth Royall.

President Roosevelt was furious. "The two Americans are guilty of treason," he told Biddle. "It seems to me that the death penalty is almost obligatory." He wanted swift justice. "I won't hand them over to any United States marshal armed with a writ of habeas corpus," he assured Biddle.[13]

The Supreme Court moved swiftly to hold a special session to hear arguments as to the constitutionality of the tribunals trying the accused saboteurs. A major focus of the arguments was the 1866 Milligan decision. Biddle insisted that the German saboteurs could not be compared with Milligan and the Civil War plotters. Kenneth Royall pleaded that the situation was similar and that the Court should follow the Milligan ruling that stated that the Constitution must apply "equally in war and peace."[14]

Meanwhile, Supreme Court Justice Owen Roberts had told his fellow justices that Biddle feared that Roosevelt would execute the Germans no matter what the Court decided. This, he feared, would have seriously undermined the authority of the Court and could have led to a breakdown of faith in the U.S. judicial system. Theoretically, the justices could not allow themselves to be influenced by such concerns. In fact, there is no evidence that they were. Still, the Court found that "the enemy combatant who without uniform comes secretly through the lines for the purpose of waging war by destruction of life or property" could be tried by secret military tribunals even if civilian courts were accessible.[15]

On August 8 the tribunal found the eight accused saboteurs guilty. The informant, George Dasch, despite a previous agreement with the prosecution to pardon him, was sentenced to thirty years in prison. Another of those convicted also received a long prison term. The other six were sentenced to death in the electric chair. All of the sentences were by order of President Roosevelt and were carried out on the same day the men were convicted.

Another of President Roosevelt's World War II actions has been criticized as violating the Constitution. Soon after the Japanese attacked Pearl Harbor, Roosevelt issued Executive Order 9066 authorizing the roundup of Japanese Americans on the West Coast. More than 110,000 men, women, and children were transported inland to internment camps and held there throughout the war.

The 1943 Supreme Court upheld the action. "Whatever views we may entertain regarding the loyalty to this country of the citizens of Japanese ancestry," they wrote, "we cannot reject as unfounded the judgment of the military authorities and of Congress that there were disloyal members of that population."[16] President Roosevelt's reason for the Japanese-American internment was fear that Japanese-American citizens might be loyal to Japan and that there might be saboteurs among them. The vast majority of the American public approved this action. The sneak attack on Pearl Harbor was cited to justify it, but there also may have been racism involved in both the decision and the support.

Forty-five years later, President Ronald Reagan apologized to Japanese Americans. Nevertheless, in 1998, three years before the terrorist attack on September 11, Chief Justice of the Supreme Court William Rehnquist wrote in his book *All the Laws But One* that "there is no reason to think that future wartime presidents will act differently from . . . Roosevelt, or that future justices of the Supreme Court will decide questions differently from their predecessors." Rehnquist added that "it is neither desirable nor is it remotely likely that civil liberty will occupy as favored a position in wartime as it does in peacetime."[17]

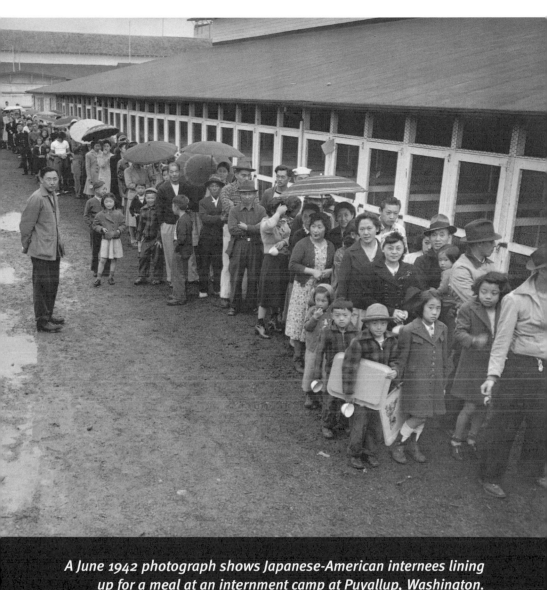

A June 1942 photograph shows Japanese-American internees lining up for a meal at an internment camp at Puyallup, Washington.

As victory seemed certain for American forces in the war in Iraq in April 2003, many peace activists in the United States were still questioning the president's authority to take such action. Despite the fact that in the autumn of the previous year Congress had voted him authorization to deploy military forces as he saw fit, they were appalled by the bombing raids which had resulted in the deaths of possibly thousands of innocent civilians. They also believed that the president lacked the authority to take military action without a declaration of war by Congress.

However, this was not the first time that Congress had relinquished its responsibility to wage war by granting special powers to the president. In 1964, the Gulf of Tonkin Resolution enacted by Congress had granted similar powers to President Lyndon Johnson. Passed following an alleged attack on two U.S. destroyers in the early years of the Vietnam War, the resolution gave Johnson the power to take any action necessary to oppose North Vietnamese aggression. Congress had been told that the attack was unprovoked. It was later revealed that the two American ships had been aiding South Vietnamese military operations against the North Vietnamese. However, the measure was repealed by Congress in 1970.

Congress was still concerned in 1973. It "felt it needed more control over the Executive Branch and the power of the President in actions other than a Declared War." It passed the War Powers Act, which "prohibits the President from waging war beyond 60 days without Congressional approval." Although President Bush had received congressional approval for U.S. military actions in Afghanistan following the September 11 terrorist attacks, his critics accused him of not complying with the sixty-day requirement of the War Powers Act, or with the thirty-day extension it allows when there are extenuating circumstances.[18]

Administration supporters, however, have argued that in times of peril strong leadership is needed. They say that the United States is engaged in a war against terrorism and to tie our leader's hands with legal niceties would be to risk further loss of American lives and property. Supporters also point out that eight U.S. presidents since Franklin Roosevelt had put American troops in harm's way without a formal declaration of war. Under Presidents Truman and Eisenhower, more than 2 million troops served in Korea.

Approximately 37,000 died. In July 1958, Eisenhower sent 5,000 marines to Lebanon to help put down a rebellion. President Kennedy sent the first American servicemen to Vietnam in the early 1960s. In all, 2.7 million Americans served in Vietnam and almost 60,000 gave their lives.

In 1962, President Kennedy also ordered 4,000 troops into Laos to help put down a pro-Communist rebellion. In April 1965, President Johnson ordered 14,000 U.S. troops to the Dominican Republic to support a military coup that unseated a left-wing government. In 1970, President Nixon sent several thousand combat troops into Cambodia.

President Ronald Reagan sent 1,400 U.S. marines as peacekeepers to Lebanon in 1983. Two hundred forty-one of them were killed by a terrorist suicide bomb. Later that year he authorized the invasion of the tiny Caribbean island of Grenada by about 1,900 marines, 19 of whom died. Three years later Reagan ordered the bombing of Libya by American war-planes. An invasion force of 27,000 U.S. troops was sent to Panama in 1989 by the first president George Bush to overthrow the government and capture Panama's president, Manuel Ortega, an accomplice of regional drug dealers. Twenty-three Americans, and thousands of Panamanians, were killed during the invasion. Between 1990 and 1991, Bush deployed more than half a million U.S. military personnel to the Persian Gulf to force Iraq out of Kuwait. Two hundred ninety-nine Americans died. Later, President Bush dispatched 25,000 troops to Somalia as a peacekeeping force. Eighteen were killed in a firefight in 1993 after Bill Clinton became president. Clinton sent U.S. troops to Haiti in 1994, and several hundred remained there for the next five years. In 1999, Clinton ordered bombing raids by U.S. planes on Serbia.

Each of these military actions was viewed by the presidents who authorized them as necessary to the interests of the United States. In general, they reflected the conviction of a majority of lawmakers in both political parties that we are part of a global world in which despo-tism and aggression must sometimes be dealt with as a threat to democracy. Following the terrorist attack of September 11, the threat of a regime hostile to the United States in Iraq possessing terrorist weapons which might be used in another such assault was the reason President George W. Bush sent upwards of a quarter-million troops to war in the Middle East.

CHAPTER FIVE

KEEPING THE VIGIL

A terrorism alert is not a signal to stop your life.
It is a call to be vigilant—to know that your government
is on high alert, and to add your eyes and ears to find
and stop those who want to do us harm.

President George W. Bush,
November 8, 2001

Shortly after September 11, high-ranking government officials began urging ordinary citizens to be on the alert for future terrorist activity, to exercise vigilance, to share their concerns with friends or neighbors, and to warn airport authorities, local police, and federal officials of suspicious activities and of individuals whose appearance and/or actions made them seem questionable. President Bush urged citizens to "know that your government is on high alert, and to add your eyes and ears to find and stop those who want to do us harm."[1] The government felt that it was important that citizens participate in safeguarding their country as much as possible.

By mid-January 2002, the FBI had received more than half a million calls concerning possible terrorist threats from concerned citizens. Local law enforcement agencies received thousands more. Critics worried that such vigilance might "make America a country of tattletales, a place where innocent residents need to be on guard against false allegations." They also worried that the so-called national neighborhood watch encouraged by national leaders might lead to ethnic profiling. The watch had "few guidelines" and had "borne few results" according to the *Christian Science Monitor*. Elliot Mincberg, legal director for People for the American Way in Washington, asked "will it go too far?"[2]

■ ■ ■ ■ ■ ■ ■ ■ ■ ■ ■ ■ ■ ■ ■ ■ ■ ■ **NEIGHBORHOOD WATCH**

Fifty million people from all over the United States participate in National Neighborhood Watch, a volunteer program in the war against terrorism. Before September 11 it was a grassroots organization mainly devoted to fighting crime and ridding local areas of drug dealers. It was founded in 1972 by Dean Keuter Jr. of the National Sheriffs' Association who now redefines its aim as "fighting terrorism on the neighborhood level."[3]

That goal was given encouragement on March 6, 2002, when Attorney General John Ashcroft announced plans to add $2 million to federal funding of the program in order to double the number of local chapters. "Through the Neighborhood Watch program," Ashcroft said, "we will weave a seamless web of prevention of terrorism that brings together citizens and law enforcement."[4]

Neighborhood Watch is a part of Citizen Corps, which is itself a section of the USA Freedom Corps. An umbrella organization with several components, Freedom Corps' overall mission is preventing, or reacting, to terrorism. President Bush defines it as "a chance to serve your nation."[5] He believes the Freedom Corps will prolong the patriotic and community-focused attitudes that emerged after the September 11 attack.

The Neighborhood Watch program had been in existence for nearly 30 years prior to September 11, mainly as a cooperative measure to rid neighborhoods of crime. After the attacks, the organization redefined itself, expanding its philosophy to include antiterrorism.

■■■■■■■■■■■■■■■■■ USA FREEDOM CORPS

Freedom Corps follows in the tradition of President John Kennedy's Peace Corps and President Bill Clinton's AmeriCorps. Like them, it asks Americans to volunteer their time and effort to work with various programs. The difference is that its major concern has to do with terrorism. President Bush has urged each citizen to devote two years, or four thousand hours, to Freedom Corps community service over their lifetimes.

Along with Citizen Corps, AmeriCorps and Peace Corps were incorporated into Freedom Corps. Disaster preparedness was made a key part of the AmeriCorps mission. The Peace Corps was charged with creating crisis teams of volunteers to help rebuild Afghanistan. Citizen Corps broke down into Community Emergency Response Teams, a Medical Reserve Corps made up of retired doctors and nurses, the Neighborhood Watch program, and a Terrorist Information and Prevention System (Operation TIPS), scheduled to begin in ten U.S. cities in August 2002.

■■■■■■■■■■■■■■■■■■■■■■■ OPERATION TIPS

The pilot stage of Operation TIPS was to involve one million workers. These would be truck drivers, letter carriers, train conductors, ship captains, utility employees, and others whose jobs positioned them to spot unusual events or suspicious activity. Every participant would be given an Operation TIPS sticker for his workplace, vehicle, mailbag, or some other handy location. It would have a toll-free number to a hot line routing calls to the proper law enforcement agency.

Operation TIPS ran into a roadblock during the hearings on making the Office of Homeland Security a cabinet-level department. Scheduled to be part of that department,

Operation TIPS was opposed on the grounds that it encouraged American citizens to spy on other citizens. As might be expected, the ACLU and other civil liberties groups condemned the program. Less predictably, it was opposed by the U.S. Postal Service and some federal lawmakers, including Dick Armey, Republican leader of the House of Representatives. By November 2002, following the House of Representatives' passage of a Homeland Security Bill, which specifically forbid implementation of Operation Tips, the Justice Department had quietly dropped the program.

■■■■■■■ "HOMELAND DEFENSE STARTS AT HOME"

Neighborhood Watch chapters are concerned with their own immediate residential and business area. Reports are made to the local police, or sheriff, or—on rare occasions—to the local FBI office. Its mission was summed up by thirty-three-year-old Butch Kinerney, a founding member of the South Riding Neighborhood Watch in Loudoun County, Virginia. "Our little saying is, 'Homeland defense starts at home,'" says Kinerney. "South Riding is certainly not a terrorism hot spot. But we know who belongs there and who doesn't belong there."[6]

The mission is backed up by the National Neighborhood Watch Institute located in Southern California. They offer, at a minimum cost of twenty-seven dollars apiece, large street signs proclaiming that "We Support HOMELAND SECURITY." In red, white, and blue, the signs display a map of the United States with the warning that "All suspicious persons and activities are immediately reported to our Law Enforcement Agency."[7]

Some Neighborhood Watch groups wear orange hats and designate themselves as Orange Hat Patrols. Others don Neighborhood Watch polo shirts. Not all members are sure that either the hats, the shirts, or the Watch itself are really effective against terrorism. Peter Rothschild, a forty-five-year-old computer engineer who belongs to the Capitol Hill patrol in Washington, D.C., asks if terrorists are "going to stay out of the neighborhood because of Orange Hats? I have to wonder."[8]

■■■■■■■■■■■■■■■■ A CLIMATE OF SUSPICION

Reacting to fears that Neighborhood Watch might use racial profiling, Rothschild denies that his group might focus on innocent Arabs, or Muslims. "We're too open-minded to be racial profilers," he insists. In their Washington neighborhood, he adds, "If you see a guy in a turban, he's probably the ambassador."[9]

Hikmat Beaini, a Lebanese-American lawyer with the Fairfax County Human Rights Commission, has a different view. When he took his children on a trolley tour of Washington, the driver subjected him to questioning about his national origin. Beaini replied that he was a U.S. citizen—period. Two of the tourists got off the trolley, and throughout the ride the other passengers stared at Beaini and his children. He fears that if there is another attack against America, citizens of Middle Eastern origin are "going to pay the price."[10]

Some of them already are, according to the Washington-based Council on American-Islamic Relations (CAIR). The organization has received more than 1,700 complaints of bias incidents since September 11. Arabs and Muslims in San Francisco have been a particular target. Amatullah Almarwani of that city's Islamic Center reports a phone call that "informed me that there was a bullet waiting for my head, and the head of my child." Jill Tregor, executive director of

Intergroup Clearinghouse, reports that "in the Bay Area, we've had people beaten up so badly that they've ended up in the hospital with concussions. We've had families forced from their housing. We've had kids scared to go to school. Vandalism. Death threats." Across the nation, according to CAIR, the majority of such bias incidents go unreported.[11]

Many of the unreported incidents have to do with the climate of suspicion and fear that Muslim Americans feel has been created by the activities of Neighborhood Watch. Heightened tensions, say spokespersons for Arab-American groups, have already led to hundreds of mistaken tips that have led FBI agents and police to harass innocent Muslim citizens. "It gives me a very insecure feeling," complains M. Siddique Sheikh, chairman of the Pakistan American Business Association. "I feel like I want to hide behind the closet. That is not the way I want to see my children."[12]

■■■■■■■■■■■■■■■■■■■■■■ **MIXED MESSAGES**
U.S. government authorities from the top down have made continuing efforts to alleviate the climate of suspicion and to warn the public against anti-Muslim or anti-Arab bias. President Bush, Attorney General Ashcroft, and other cabinet members have visited mosques and consulted with leaders of Middle Eastern ethnic and religious organizations. The Justice Department's civil rights division has held forums across the country on bias and hate crimes. Many Arab, Muslim, and Sikh activists have praised the government for moving quickly and forcefully to hold down bias activity.

Nevertheless, many Muslims and others don't feel secure. They fear that if they report incidents of bias to the authorities, that might result in retaliation by the government itself. The detention and questioning of thousands of Arabs and Muslims by law enforcement agencies have raised the level of suspicion. "With some Muslims, there's a sense that 'if I report [discrimination] to the government and get in their system, I'll be constantly harassed,'" according to Joshua Salaam, civil rights coordinator for CAIR.[13]

Such fears were not calmed by the release on March 6, 2002, of a Citizens' Preparedness Guide by the National Crime Prevention Council with some financing by the U.S. Justice Department. The guide urges citizens to call the FBI if they witness "a pattern of suspicious activity."[14] It advises that "you know what is normal for your neighborhood, workplace and daily routines. If a behavior or event seems to be outside the norm or is frightening, let law enforcement authorities know."[15]

Ziad Asali, president of the American-Arab Anti-Discrimination Committee said of the preparedness guide-book, there is "nothing wrong with the idea of neighbors being watchful of each other. But," he added, "if it is by implication or design to be watching out for activities of Arab Americans or Muslim Americans, it's hard to see how this will serve the fight against terrorism. . . . This would poison the atmosphere."[16]

■ ■ ■ ■ ■ ■ ■ ■ ■ ■ ■ ■ ■ ■ ■ ■ **BEYOND WATCHFULNESS**

Shortly after September 11 a survey revealed that 82 percent of those queried said they would lead an attack against terrorists trying to take control of a plane. The problem is how accurate the perception might be of who is, and who is not, a terrorist. Too often, say Muslim leaders, such vigilance has led to bias incidents. The same is true on the ground of programs like Neighborhood Watch. Along with the Citizens' Preparedness Guide, these add up to the climate that has led ACLU president Nadine Strossen to speak of "unconstructive fear-mongering" encouraging ethnic and racial profiling.[17] On the other hand, homeland security officials believe that a vigilant population is necessary to the safety of all Americans.

■■■■■■■■■■■■■■■■■■■■ DIRTY INFORMERS

In March 2002 the Office of Homeland Security established a system to warn citizens about the possibility of a terrorist attack. The decision to issue warnings under this system is based on intelligence information from the FBI, the CIA, and other government agencies, some of it obtained from informers with questionable backgrounds despite restrictions that were placed on these agents to use such informers. (Restrictions on gathering such data were placed on these agencies, specifically the CIA, by Congress in 1995. Agents in the field were forbidden to recruit informers with questionable backgrounds without approval from top agency management.)

Many Americans, including human rights groups, were appalled at soliciting the cooperation of such people, some of whom had been involved in human rights abuses or criminal or terrorist activities. However, it is just such *dirty informers,* as they are known, who are most likely to have access to the details of plots against the United States. In 2002, in the annual congressional intelligence authorization bill, the restrictions were lifted, a move regarded as key to learning the details of terrorist attacks—and possibly preventing them—before they could take place.

BEEFING UP THE
■■■■■■■■■■■■ OFFICE OF HOMELAND SECURITY

Evaluating intelligence information, and deciding if warnings of possible terrorism should be issued to the public, was a key function of the Office of Homeland Security. This was a particularly difficult task in the aftermath of September 11. It involved coordinating data from a multitude of agencies, including not only the FBI, CIA, and Justice Department but also the Immigration and Naturalization Service, the Customs Service, the Coast Guard, the Federal Emergency Management Agency, and others. Furthermore, collecting, combining, and evaluating the data had to be done at top speed in order to warn the public of impending attacks in time to take defensive action.

In the first months following the September 11 attack, the Office of Homeland Security erred on the side of caution. When warnings were issued and no attacks took place, the public began to take them less seriously. Critics accused the administration of spreading fear unnecessarily. In response, and in order to better coordinate intelligence gathering and security operations, in midsummer of 2002, Congress acted on a request by President Bush to create legislation that would raise the Office of Homeland Security to a cabinet-level department, which would incorporate the various agencies involved in protecting the United States.

■■■■■■■■■■■■■■■ THE COLORS OF TERROR

Prior to that, on March 12, 2002, in an effort to enable the public to judge the level of danger of a threat, a new color-coded terrorism alert system had been announced by Homeland Security director Tom Ridge. It was designed to provide a "common vocabulary" for rating the danger of terrorist attacks.[18] The ratings by color were as follows:

Green: Low risk of terrorist attacks.
Blue: Guarded condition. General risk of terrorist attacks.
Yellow: Elevated condition. Significant risk of terrorist attacks.
Orange: High risk of terrorist attacks.
Red: Severe risk of terrorist attacks.[19]

Homeland Security director Tom Ridge discusses the new color-coded U.S. threat advisory system in March 2002.

The five-level system presented advice at each level for how government and industry should react. It was also "designed to measure and evaluate terrorist threats and communicate them to the public in a timely manner," Ridge said.[20] Although the nation was at Code Yellow at the time of the announcement, critics pointed out that no specific advice was being offered to concerned citizens, among whom were those who belonged to the National Neighborhood Watch.

The criticism continued, peaking in February 2003 when a Code Orange alert was announced and accompanied by a series of warnings and, it was generally agreed later, questionable advice. When there was no incident, and the warning level was rolled back to Code Yellow, Homeland Security Secretary Tom Ridge was reproached for offering conflicting and non-specific counsel. According to *Newsweek* magazine, the decision to go to Code Orange had been based in part on bogus information from unreliable informants. Ridge's response to the criticism was a "Ready Campaign" consisting of a communication plan between family members, preparation of an emergency supply kit, and staying alert on a day-to-day basis.

■ ■ ■ ■ ■ ■ ■ ■ ■ ■ ■ ■ ■ ■ ■ ■ ■ **THE NEW DEPARTMENT**

On November 26, 2002, President Bush signed legislation creating the new cabinet-level Department of Homeland Security. Tom Ridge was put in charge of it. The Department was to reshuffle nearly 170,000 workers from twenty-two government agencies in order to bring national security concerns under one center of responsibility in order to more efficiently safeguard the American people against acts of terrorism.

Despite some organizational problems in its early days, the Department of Homeland Security began its work in earnest in May 2003. Simulated terrorist attacks were set up to formulate procedures to guard against the real thing in Seattle and Chicago. At a cost of $16 million, the attacks began with a bogus dirty bomb discharging fake toxic smoke in an industrial section of South Seattle. Similar scenes were repeated in Chicago. Homeland Security Secretary Tom Ridge pronounced the exercise very useful in gauging the effectiveness of responses to terrorist attacks and revising plans to improve them. Critics pointed out that since the public knew it was a simulation, rather than a real attack, there was actually no way of judging how people would react and what responses would be effective under real-life terrorist attack conditions. That, of course, will be the question with which the Department of Homeland Security must wrestle as the threat of terrorism persists.

CHAPTER SIX

THE POW CONTROVERSY

And let there be no doubt, the treatment of the detainees in Guantánamo Bay is proper, it's humane, it's appropriate, and it's fully consistent with international conventions. No detainee has been harmed, no detainee has been mistreated in any way. And the numerous articles, statements, questions, allegations, and breathless reports on television are undoubtedly by people who are either uninformed, misinformed or poorly informed.

From Secretary of Defense Donald H. Rumsfeld's January 22, 2002, statement denying charges of mistreatment of detainees at Camp X-Ray, Guantánamo Bay

Soon after the invasion of Afghanistan began, al Qaeda and Taliban prisoners taken by the Northern Alliance were turned over to American forces. U.S. troops also took prisoners. Among all these prisoners, some were identified as having intelligence information regarding both the September 11 attack and the ongoing conflict with terrorism in Afghanistan and elsewhere. Some of these individuals were thought to have information regarding possible future plans for attacks against the United States. Those prisoners that were believed to have such information were transferred to the Camp X-Ray prison at the Guantánamo Bay U.S. military base in Cuba for further interrogation. Many human rights groups protested the transfer of these prisoners as well as their treatment during the transfer and after they reached the base.

■ ■ ■ ■ ■ ■ ■ ■ ■ ■ ■ ■ ■ ■ ■ ■ ■ ■ GROWING CONTROVERSY

The controversy surrounding the treatment of al Qaeda and Taliban prisoners at Camp X-Ray involved a disagreement over their status. The Bush administration said that they did not qualify for treatment as prisoners of war (POWs) because they did not meet the four requirements in Article 4, Section 2 of the Geneva Convention on the Treatment of Prisoners of War signed and agreed to by the United States in 1949. The article defined a combatant as a person being under the control of a superior, wearing a recognizable uniform, carrying arms openly, and acting according to the "laws and customs of war." President Bush pointed out that "al Qaeda is not a known military. These are killers, these are terrorists, they know no countries." Defense Secretary Rumsfeld agreed. "They will not be characterized as prisoners of war, because that is not what they are. They're terrorists."[1]

■ ■ ■ ■ ■ ■ ■ ■ ■ ■ ■ ■ ■ ■ ■ A QUESTION OF DEFINITION

In February 2002 the White House softened its position. It announced that the principles of the Geneva Convention would apply to Taliban and Afghan detainees. Administration spokesperson Ari Fleischer said that the change was because "the President believes in the Geneva Convention and its important principles."[2] However, this did not mean that Taliban prisoners would have POW status, and it did not apply to al Qaeda prisoners.

The reasoning behind this was spelled out by Secretary Rumsfeld. He maintained that obtaining information from detainees to prevent future acts of terrorism against the people of the United States was a clear priority for the Pentagon. The warden at Camp X-ray, Colonel Terry Carrico, put it differently. He said it was necessary to maintain "positive control" over the prisoners. Retired army major general Bill

Nash, a senior fellow at the Council on Foreign Relations, said this meant "imposing on them a psychological sense of isolation, domination and futility, and trying to establish the conditions by which you can reward them for information, as oppose to punish them."[3]

The detainees were in "legal limbo," according to Michael F. Noone, professor of military law at Catholic University. He insisted it was urgent that the United States screen the prisoners to separate out terrorists and declare the others POWs. When Defense Secretary Rumsfeld was asked why this had not been done, he cited legal technicalities and added that "the process of gathering the intelligence information has not been concluded."[4]

■■■■■■■■■■■■■■■■ **CAMP X-RAY CONDITIONS**

In January 2002 the Defense Department released photographs of prisoners from Afghanistan arriving at Camp X-Ray. As described in *The New York Times*, the photographs "showed some of the prisoners kneeling before their captors, their legs in shackles, their hands bound in manacles, their mouths covered by surgical masks and their eyes blinded by large goggles with black tape." The pictures aroused a storm of protests from foreign governments and human rights groups. The International Committee of the Red Cross issued a statement saying the United States might have violated the Geneva Convention rules against making a spectacle of prisoners. Amnesty International viewed the pictures as evidence of "classic techniques employed to break the spirit of individuals" for purposes of interrogation. Deploring such treatment, Javier Solana, the European Union foreign policy chief, pointed out that "changing our values and our way of life would be terrorism's first victory."[5]

In this January 2002 photo, al Qaeda and Taliban detainees captured in Afghanistan sit in a holding area under the surveillance of U.S. military police at Camp X-Ray at Guantánamo Bay Naval Base, Cuba.

Secretary Rumsfeld defended the transportation procedures. "I haven't found a single scrap of any kind of information that suggests that anyone has been treated anything other than humanely," he insisted. "When they are being moved from place to place," he asked, "will they be restrained in a way so that they are less likely to be able to kill an American soldier? You bet. Is it inhumane to do that? No. Would it be stupid to do anything else? Yes."[6]

Criticism of the handling of prisoners at Camp X-Ray continued when news reports indicated that they were confined "in small cages with chain-link sides, concrete floors and metal roofs."[7] The Geneva Convention mandates that prisoners of war may not be held in close confinement except where necessary to safeguard their health.

The criticisms led to an investigation of conditions at Camp X-Ray on January 26, 2002, by a twenty-five-member congressional group made up of three senators and twenty-two members of the House of Representatives. On the whole, the lawmakers found that international criticism of the prison was unwarranted. Representative John Mica of Florida thought conditions were "too good" for those being held at Guantánamo. Senator James Inhofe of Oklahoma said the circumstances of their imprisonment "were better than they deserve. We're dealing with terrorists here."[8] Senator Daniel Inouye of Hawaii found conditions at Camp X-Ray "in many ways superior" to those at Oahu prison in Hawaii, which he used to visit as a prosecutor. He noted that each detainee was housed in an 8- by 8-foot (2.4- by 2.4-meter) cell enclosed by wire mesh. The cells had awnings to shield them from the sun, as well as mattresses 4 or 5 inches (10 or 13 centimeters) thick. Each twelve-cell compound had three portable toilets and three shower stalls. As for food, Senator Inouye said he believed that "their noon meal was a little better than the noon meal we had on the plane."[9]

■■■■■■■■■■■■■■■■■■■ THE HUNGER STRIKE

On February 26, 2002, a Camp X-Ray prisoner fashioned a turban from his bed sheet and began to pray. A guard, who later claimed to have been acting out of concern for the prisoner's safety, pulled the makeshift turban from the Muslim's head as he was praying. The man protested, and soon other prisoners were protesting with him. Within two days, two hundred of the three hundred prisoners at Guantánamo were staging a hunger strike. Its aims went beyond the initial demands that their religion be respected by their captors to protests against their continued detention, the refusal of authorities to clarify their legal status, and the uncertainty of their future at Camp X-Ray.

The hunger strike attracted worldwide attention on how the United States was treating the prisoners at Guantánamo. Middle Eastern and other countries as well as international human rights groups claimed that the treatment was inhuman. Authorities at Guantánamo could claim with some justification that the criticism was unfair. They had provided prisoners with skullcaps, copies of the Koran (the Muslim bible), Muslim clergy to lead prayer services, and specially prepared meals in keeping with Muslim dietary laws. The Guantánamo command also defended itself against charges of having been insensitive to the detainees' religion by shaving off their beards, which is forbidden by Muslim law. They pointed out that it had been a health measure against lice and the spread of disease, and had been done for the well-being of the prisoners themselves.

TORTURE AND SURVIVAL

Some human rights groups said that the treatment of detainees at Guantánamo Bay constitutes a form of torture. The Bush administration denied that it has ever used, or ever will use, torture. Secretary of State Colin Powell pointed out that obeying the Geneva Convention, that forbids torture, could protect U.S. soldiers who become POWs from mistreatment by their captors. Nevertheless, polls indicate that almost one third of Americans were unconcerned and would support some use of torture. Harvard law professor Alan Dershowitz, usually a critic of Bush administration policy, argues for torture in cases of threats to national security if "torture warrants" are issued by a court and there is official oversight of the torture.[10] *The Washington Post* writer Walter Pincus reasons that "there are a lot of kinds of pressures that under, you know, international law may be described as quote 'torture' that really aren't."[11]

Human rights organizations like Amnesty International were disturbed by this. Article 17 of the Geneva Convention decrees that "no physical or mental torture, nor any other form of coercion, may be inflicted on prisoners of war to secure from them information of any kind whatever. Prisoners of war who refuse to answer may not be threatened, insulted, or exposed to any unpleasant or disadvantageous treatment of any kind."[12] There was concern that U.S. treatment of detainees at Guantánamo Bay might overstep these bounds.

Can torture be morally justified? Consider the following scenario:

A terrorist bomb has been placed in a central terminal used by tens of thousands of people each day. An informant has alerted authorities to the plot, but does not know which terminal was targeted. He has also identified one of those involved in the scheme.

This person is taken prisoner and interrogated. He refuses to answer any questions. The bomb could go off at any minute, and the loss of life would be great. Is torture justified to obtain information from the terrorist to prevent this tragedy?

There are arguments pro and con. In Sri Lanka when three terrorists were caught and refused to talk, one was killed in front of the other two who then revealed the location of explosives set to blow up large numbers of people. On the other hand, former CIA agent Robert Baer, author of *See No Evil,* speaks of a case of torture and death in Lebanon that resulted in "essentially worthless" information. Baer believes that "usually physical torture does not work (although) psychological torture, over a long period of time, may break somebody."[13]

Al Qaeda detainees, who might be likely to have knowledge of future terrorist operations against the United States, would be the most likely subjects for such treatment. It would, however, violate a section of the Geneva Convention, which says that irregular forces such as al Qaeda "shall enjoy the protection of the present Convention until such time as their status has been determined by a competent tribunal."[14]

Beyond the legalities, Amnesty International, Human Rights Watch, and other organizations believe there are humanitarian principles at stake. Many Americans, including some who are members of our government, agree. Torture, they believe, is not only inhumane. It is un-American.

Nevertheless, after the hunger strike, Guantánamo officials changed the Camp X-Ray rules to allow prisoners to wear do-it-yourself turbans. Military commander Brigadier General Michael Lehnert made a point of reassuring the prisoners that steps were being taken to improve their conditions. "Within five weeks, all of you will be moved to another place near by, where you will each have a bed, running water, a sink, and a toilet," he informed them on March 8. "There will be an exercise area and conditions will be better for you." He added that "we have also assigned one senior guard who will pass through each of the cell blocks to determine your needs and to ensure that you are being treated fairly."[15]

By this time only twenty-one of the prisoners were still on a hunger strike. General Lehnert read to them from the Koran in an effort to convince them to give up their protest. Marine captain Alan Crouch assured reporters that "we're certainly not going to allow them to harm themselves or starve."[16] By the end of March, the hunger strike was an on-again, off-again tactic. Some who had been on strike started eating. Some who had been eating began refusing food. Military spokesman Major James Bell said that "we don't have a 100 percent method of confirming whether or not an individual has eaten."[17] Although the British Broadcasting Company (BBC), the official radio and TV network of Great Britain, reported that "the number of detainees on hunger strike has doubled," U.S. authorities insisted it had declined.[18]

■■■■■■■■■■■■■■■■ **THE AMERICAN TALIBAN**

As of September 2002, one year after the terrorist attack on the United States, more than 450 accused al Qaeda and Taliban fighters were being held at the Guantánamo base and faced either military tribunals or indefinite detention. Their undefined status was protested by some foreign governments as well as by ordinary citizens in Middle Eastern countries and elsewhere.

Many of the captives held at Guantánamo had come from countries other than Afghanistan. Some of these countries were asking for their return. The Bush administration, while not denying such requests outright, was not granting them. The U.S. position was that terrorists should be tried by a U.S. tribunal and, if found guilty, should be put to death. However, this only applied to non-U.S. citizens. The case of John Walker Lindh focused the resentment of other nations on this stipulation.

Lindh, a nineteen-year-old American from California, had joined the Taliban, been trained at a camp in Afghanistan run by al Qaeda, fought in the front lines against the Northern Alliance, and was taken prisoner by Americans and held in a fortress prison in northern Afghanistan along with hundreds of other Taliban soldiers. Here, CIA agent Mike Spann interrogated Lindh at length while his partner filmed the procedure. Lindh was unresponsive, and in an exchange between the two agents, the partner warned that Lindh needed "to decide if he wants to live or die." He added that if Lindh didn't talk, they would leave him there in the filthy prison for the rest of his short life. Lindh still said nothing. A little later, according to an interview Lindh gave *Newsweek*, "someone either pulled a knife or threw a grenade at the guards or got their guns, and started shooting." Another rebellion erupted. Spann was beaten, shot, and killed by the mob. Lindh was shot in the leg.[19]

When Northern Alliance forces tried to restore order, the prisoners regrouped in the basement of the fortress and resisted. Lindh was with them. After U.S. warplanes dropped bombs on the rebellious prisoners, eighty-five of the rebels surrendered. John Walker Lindh was one of them.

■ ■ ■ ■ ■ ■ ■ ■ ■ ■ ■ CHARGES AND COUNTERCHARGES

There are two different interpretations of what happened next. The U.S. government claims that Lindh was unrepentant. "It was a mistake," they quoted him as saying, "to attack governments that are supported by the United States . . . it was more effective to attack the head of the snake."[20] Government attorneys assigned to prosecute Lindh claim that he "maintained his allegiance to enemies of this country."[21]

Lindh's defense attorneys claimed that he expressed regret about the September 11 attacks to his interrogators, telling them that he was "very ashamed due to the high death toll."[22] Federal prosecutors confirmed that this was true. Defense attorneys charged that Lindh had been "tortured" into making self-incriminating statements while in custody.[23] They asserted that he had asked for a lawyer and was told none was available. "For fifty-four days, the United States government . . . kept John Lindh away from a lawyer," according to James J. Brosnahan, Lindh's lead defense attorney.[24]

Prosecutors denied that Lindh had been ill-treated. Granting that battle zone conditions were difficult, they argued that Lindh's treatment was "comparable to or better than U.S. soldiers."[25] The responsibility for his situation, prosecutors said, was his own. "Lindh was treated as a potentially dangerous detainee given his suspected affiliation with a terrorist organization," they said in papers filed with a U.S. court.[26] Attorney General Ashcroft insisted Lindh "chose to waive his right to an attorney, both orally and in writing, before his statement to the FBI."[27]

John Walker Lindh was sentenced to twenty years in prison as part of an agreement reached in July 2002 under which he pled guilty to one count of supplying services to the Taliban and a criminal information charge that he carried a rifle and two hand grenades while fighting against the U.S.-backed Northern Alliance.

■ ■ ■ ■ ■ ■ ■ ■ ■ ■ ■ ■ ■ **PUNISHMENT DISCREPANCIES**

Because Lindh was an American citizen, he could not be tried by a military tribunal. He was held in a civilian prison in Virginia rather than at the POW camp in Guantánamo. While pretrial arguments were proceeding, there were outcries from foreign governments regarding the discrepancy in the charges faced by Lindh and the possible charges against foreigners held by the United States. None of the ten offenses with which Lindh was charged carried a death penalty.

On July 15, 2002, as a result of a plea bargain with prosecutors, Lindh pled guilty to two of the charges against him. In return, prosecutors dropped the other charges. On October 4 he received the maximum sentence on both counts for a total of twenty years in prison.

The discrepancy between Lindh's punishment and the possibility that some al Qaeda detainees may be sentenced to death by military tribunals has drawn protests from countries whose citizens are being held by the United States. Many of the detainees were not native Afghans, but, like Lindh, had gone to Afghanistan as volunteers to fight with the Taliban and/or al Qaeda. Some of the countries from which they came had outlawed the death penalty. Their governments accused the United States of regarding a foreigner's life as less valuable than that of an American.

Article 3, Part I of the Geneva Conventions relative to the treatment of prisoners of war forbids "the carrying out of executions without previous judgment pronounced by a regularly constituted court affording all the judicial guarantees which are recognized as indispensable by civilized peoples."[28]

It follows that if a foreign national is sentenced to death, the United States might find itself facing charges of violating international law. Such charges might seriously affect the nation's ability to effectively conduct foreign policy. While many in the administration, and many private citizens as well, feel that it is only just that terrorists should be punished, there are also those who feel that other countries' perception of the United States as unjust cannot be ignored. They pointed out that President Bush himself had often said that our nation coexists in a global context. Sensitivity to that context, they say, may be necessary to ensure allies in our war against terrorism.

CHAPTER SEVEN

PATRIOTIC CRITICS

To those who scare peace-loving people with phantoms of lost liberty, my message is this: Your tactics only aid terrorists, for they erode our national unity and diminish our resolve. They give ammunition to America's enemies and pause to America's friends.

Attorney General John Ashcroft answers critics of the administration while testifying before the Senate Judiciary Committee on December 7, 2001

Few doubted the sincerity of those in the Bush administration when they took steps to protect the nation and its people from further acts of terrorism. President George W. Bush, Attorney General John Ashcroft, Homeland Security Director Tom Ridge, Secretary of State Colin Powell, Secretary of Defense Donald Rumsfeld, and other leaders acted according to their perception of present and future threats to our safety. Said Attorney General Ashcroft a few months after the attack, "On the morning of September 11, as the United States came under attack, I was in an airplane with several members of the Justice Department en route to Milwaukee in the skies over the Great Lakes. From that moment, at the command of the President of the United States, I began to mobilize the resources of the Department of Justice toward one single overarching and overriding objective: to save innocent lives from further acts of terrorism."[1] The Bush administration acted decisively despite the criticism that they got, and the criticism that they could anticipate. It has repeatedly said that it does not want to violate civil rights. However, homeland security must come first, it believes. Poll after poll shows that a majority of the American people agree.

Specifically, U. S. citizens have focused concern on security since the early days of the war in Iraq when the national fear level was raised and lowered, and raised and lowered by announcements of next-to-highest and highest color levels of terrorism alerts. Conflicting announcements involving the use of duct tape and other precautionary measures increased confusion along with fear. Opponents of the war accused the administration of neglecting legitimate security concerns, and of having no plan to deal with an attack because of their preoccupation with Iraq.

■ ■ ■ ■ ■ ■ ■ ■ ■ ■ ■ ■ ■ ■ ■ **AGGRESSION OR DEFENSE?**
"The president is commander in chief of the armed forces," Anthony Lewis reminded readers in an op-ed piece in *The New York Times*, "and in wartime people tend to fall in behind the commander." Lewis added that "President Bush's high level of public support [following September 11] is not surprising."[2] However, Lewis sees a danger in such popularity. His concern, as well as that of others, often focuses on what many consider the president's overly aggressive foreign policy and use of U.S. troops. The president had declared a total war on terrorism. He sent U.S. troops to Afghanistan and elsewhere. He accused North Korea, Iran, and Iraq of constituting an axis of evil—relating them to al Qaeda. He accused Iraq of developing weapons of mass destruction and called for a war against Iraq that

In April 2002 a U.S. Army Blackhawk helicopter lands near a group of U.S. Marines and their Filipino counterparts at Ternate, Cavite province, in the Philippines. The troops were placed there to combat global terrorism.

could involve as many as half a million American troops. These actions are cited by critics as evidence of an overly gung ho foreign policy.

Answering such charges, the president has stood firm. "As long as there is al Qaeda influence anywhere we will help the host countries rout them and bring them to justice," he said.[3] By mid-March of 2002, President Bush had committed American military forces to the Philippines, Yemen, and the Republic of Georgia, which was formerly part of the Soviet Union. In each case, he, or a member of his administration, explained why the troops were sent. In the Philippines, Abu Sayyaf, the leading guerrilla group, had held two U.S. citizens hostage since May 2001. There was evidence that Abu Sayyaf has al Qaeda connections. One objective of the U.S. troops was to free the hostages, one of whom was subsequently killed during a rescue attempt by U.S.-trained Philippine troops. The first contingent of 650 U.S. troops arrived in the Philippines in January 2002. When it was learned that the agreement between the United States and the Philippines gave Philippine commanders authority over U.S. soldiers, there were protests in Congress.

Forty American military personnel were flown into the former Soviet republic of Georgia on February 21, 2002. Their assignment was to "advise" local forces on tactics and weapons to use against terrorists and to launch and operate remote-control guided missiles. The targets were Chechen and Islamic militants operating in the Panski Gorge near the Georgian border with Chechnya. According to one Pentagon official, "We have a clear connection between Chechens and al Qaeda. They clearly fall under the potential targets of the global war on terrorism."[4]

In early March, 240 American soldiers arrived in Yemen and took up positions in the northern and eastern parts of the country. A year and a half earlier, in October 2000, the *U.S.S. Cole*, anchored off Yemen, fell victim to a suicide bombing. Seventeen American sailors died. U.S. intelligence sources found evidence that Osama bin Laden was behind the attack. According to one U.S. official, Yemen is a haven for thousands of Afghans who fled there after the Soviet-Afghan war and who have significant links to al Qaeda. There have been frequent clashes between so-called Afghan Arabs who belong to al Qaeda and Yemen security forces. "People ask why we're in Yemen," Defense Secretary Rumsfeld has said. "My answer is would you like Yemen to become the next Afghanistan? I think nobody wants that to happen, and goodness knows the Yemeni government does not."[5]

■■■■■■■■■■■■■■■ **CRITICISM OR DISLOYALTY?**

When Senate majority leader Democrat Tom Daschle questioned the wisdom of dispersing American troops so widely, he was denounced by Republican minority leader Trent Lott. "How dare Senator Daschle criticize President Bush while we are fighting our war on terrorism?" Senator Lott demanded.[6]

This raised the question of whether criticism is unpatriotic. President Bush had warned that the war will go on indefinitely as we root out terrorists around the world. His supporters argued that some minor short-term sacrifices of civil liberties may be necessary to maintain homeland security. His critics find that a slippery slope. "How," asks Anthony Lewis, "will we protect civil liberties in a war without end?"[7]

The Senate was not to be hushed by implications of disloyalty like that voiced by Senator Lott. The flash point for their asserting their right to criticize was Iraq. On April 28, 2002, *The New York Times* reported that the Bush administration was developing a plan for a major air campaign and ground invasion of Iraq that could involve as many as a quarter of a million U.S. troops. Although a week later the administration denied that it was planning any imminent action, National Security Adviser Condoleezza Rice admitted that "we're in consultation with our friends and allies" in regard to taking action against Iraq and "we have felt, the president felt, that it is extremely important to make clear that the status quo is not acceptable with this regime."[8] In both houses of Congress there were calls from some members of both parties demanding that President Bush explain his plans and the reasons for them to the public and that he consult with Congress before taking action.

Since taking office, the president and key members of his administration had stressed the need to rid Iraq of its leader, Saddam Hussein, and replace him with a democratic government not hostile to the United States. The most recent reason was Iraq's buildup of chemical and biological weapons, the fear that it was developing weapons of mass destruction (WMD), and Saddam's refusal to allow United Nations inspectors to investigate weapons manufacturing and storage sites as per the agreements reached with the UN following the Gulf War. Also of concern were suspicions that Iraq was cooperating with and even harboring terrorists.

■■■■■■■■■■■■■■■■■■■■■ THE "AXIS OF EVIL"
Lawmakers did not necessarily disagree with the administration's desire to topple the Hussein regime. Some did feel, however, that the president should seek congressional approval before mounting an invasion. Senator Chuck Hagel, Republican of Nebraska, went further. "We need a national dialogue," he insisted. "If the United States decides to take action against Iraq, Americans need to understand the risks and objectives." Hagel, a decorated veteran of the Vietnam War, added "that was a debate we didn't have with Vietnam."[9]

In October 2002, there was such a debate. Its result was that Congress voted to give President Bush broad powers to wage war in Iraq. As of March 2003, 150,000 Americans were in the Mid-East. Despite wide opposition both at home and abroad, the administration was poised to proceed.

Iraq, along with Iran and North Korea, had been singled out by President Bush in his January 2002 State of the Union address as part of the "axis of evil arming to threaten the peace of the world." He said that "Iraq continues to flaunt its hostility toward America and to support terror." He warned that he would "not stand by as peril draws closer and closer. The United States of America will not permit the world's most dangerous regimes to threaten us with the world's most destructive weapons."[10]

Those nations making up what the Bush administration considers the "axis of evil" was expanded on May 6 by Under Secretary of State John Bolton to include "rogue states" Syria, Libya, and Cuba. "America is determined to prevent the next wave of terror," Bolton said. "States that sponsor terror and pursue WMD (weapons of mass destruction) must stop."[11] In point of fact, Iraq would be the first such nation to be targeted as a "rogue state" by the Bush administration.

■ ■ ■ ■ THE OFFICE OF STRATEGIC INFLUENCE (OSI)

The administration was not just concerned about states that sponsored terrorism. It was also worried about the pro-terrorist and anti-American attitudes held by large numbers of people in many Middle Eastern nations, some of whose governments are allies of the United States. Following September 11, jubilation had been expressed in some Palestinian cities where the United States is regarded as an ally of Israel as well as other nations friendly to the United States such as Egypt and Saudi Arabia.

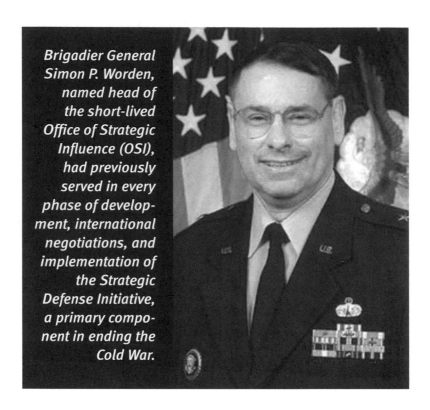

Brigadier General Simon P. Worden, named head of the short-lived Office of Strategic Influence (OSI), had previously served in every phase of development, international negotiations, and implementation of the Strategic Defense Initiative, a primary component in ending the Cold War.

In an effort to counteract this growing hostility within the Muslim world and concerned with the hostility of populations and not just governments, in October 2001 the Bush administration established a low-profile Pentagon agency called the Office of Strategic Influence (OSI) with a multi-million dollar budget. Brigadier General Simon Worden of the Air Force was put in charge of the agency. According to a senior Pentagon official, the office was set up because we were having "our butts handed to us every day in the propaganda war."[12] OSI's original purpose was to distribute information to bolster support for U.S. military actions among overseas populations, "particularly in Islamic countries."[13]

The creation of OSI was not made public until mid-February, 2002. *The New York Times,* which broke the story, revealed that General Worden's plans for OSI included the use of "disinformation and other covert activities."[14] *The Times* of London defined OSI as "a covert unit" set up "to wage an information war that could include feeding false stories to foreign media."[15] The Rendon Group, an international consulting firm with a reputation for running propaganda campaigns in Arab countries, was hired at a fee of $100,000 a month to work with OSI. The mission of OSI was defined by General Richard B. Myers, chairman of the Joint Chiefs of Staff. He said it was "putting together what we call a strategic influence campaign quickly and with the right emphasis. That's everything from psychological operations to the public affairs piece to coordinating partners in this effort with us."[16] The campaign would be aimed at countries that were both unfriendly and friendly to the United States.

Initially, objections to the OSI mission were raised within the Pentagon itself. Senior Pentagon officials worried that its powers were too broadly defined and that some of those powers might be illegal. The officials were disturbed that OSI authority covered areas such as computer network attacks, psychological warfare, so-called *black* campaigns involving deceptions that might affect allies as well as enemies, the spread of disinformation, and the military's worldwide public relations network. "This breaks down the boundaries almost completely," a senior Pentagon officer complained. Others feared that OSI put the credibility of the U.S. government at risk with the media, the public, and other governments. A second Pentagon official found being briefed on OSI plans, "scary."[17]

Many journalists were alarmed by the potential damage OSI disinformation campaigns might cause. Some pointed to the Vietnam era in which misleading briefings by the Pentagon and the spread of false information by the CIA had created what was then known as a credibility gap that caused widespread distrust of government by young people and other Americans. This had prompted Congress to pass a law forbidding the release of disinformation by the CIA and the FBI within the borders of the United States. The law did not forbid spreading disinformation abroad, however, and Defense Secretary Donald Rumsfeld admitted that the OSI would mount campaigns to mislead adversaries about potential attacks, for instance, by what he called "tactical deception." This alarmed Barbara Cochran, president of the Radio-Television News Directors Association. "In this age of global communication," she wrote in a letter to Rumsfeld, "misleading information disseminated overseas would quickly become known to U.S. news organizations. There would be no way to ensure that falsehoods told abroad would not also be told to the American public."[18]

Within a week of *The New York Times* revelation of the OSI's existence, protests had mounted. Secretary Rumsfeld responded, saying that because of the criticism, the OSI "could not function effectively. So it is being closed down."[19]

There were three reactions to the closing down of OSI. Some people thought the shutdown deprived the United States of an important capability in the war against terrorism. Some were appalled that a government entity designed to deal in lies and deception had been set up in the first place. However, a third group saw the whole episode as proof of decency and democracy in action, a well intentioned but questionable tactic abandoned under pressure by those bent on maintaining American values even when the nation was at risk.

■■■■■■■■■■■■■ MUFFLING THE NETWORKS

In October 2001, U.S. television networks broadcast two videos they had received from the Arab news channel, al Jazeera. The videos contained appeals by Osama bin Laden and his lieutenants for Muslims to rise up against U.S. targets around the world. After they were aired, national security adviser Condoleezza Rice set up a conference call with executives of the five major U.S. networks—CNN, NBC, ABC, CBS, and Fox News Channel—explaining that the Bush administration was concerned that the tapes could inflame violence against Americans at home and abroad. Reports of civilian casualties from U.S. bombings in Afghanistan could weaken the resolve of our Middle East allies, she said, and could harm homeland morale. She was also worried that the tapes could have included coded messages for al Qaeda cells around the world.

The networks were not convinced that the tapes conveyed coded messages. Such messages could be transmitted much more easily, and widely, over the Internet. Nevertheless, they agreed to cooperate with the government. CNN promised to "consider guidance from appropriate authorities" in making decisions about what it would air. Fox News owner Rupert Murdoch promised to do "whatever is our patriotic duty," adding that "a major diminution of civil liberties" was necessary because of "unpredictable but protracted terrorism within our borders." Andrew Hayward, president of CBS, called it "appropriate to explore new ways of fulfilling our responsibilities to the public."[20] Media leaders generally saw the threat to the homeland as serious and backed the administration's restrictions, but many journalists and others looked at the Bush administration's actions as serious restraints on a free press.

When the war with Iraq began, however, restrictions on the media were relaxed. Clips from al Jazeera and other Arab networks were allowed to be shown on television. Indeed, they provided some of the most striking pictorial footage of the war. Also, network and newspaper reporters were embedded with U. S. and British troops and were allowed to report from the battlefield. A handful of correspondents reported from inside Baghdad during the intensive bombing which preceded the arrival of U. S. troops in the city. Sadly, ten reporters from a variety of countries died during the days preceding the fall of Baghdad.

■■■■■■■■■■■■■■■■■■■■■■ A BALANCING ACT

Democracy in action, since September 11, has been a balancing act. Many who criticize the administration feel that in its zeal to protect homeland security, it has put the basic rights of Americans at risk. Those who back the administration believe that a nation at war against terrorism must take strong measures to protect itself first and worry about the niceties of rights and liberties later. However, these are not hard and fast positions held by any one side of the political spectrum.

Many liberals generally concerned with civil rights have relaxed their positions in the face of terrorist action. While they may question if a threat is imminent, once they are convinced that it is, they do not suggest that the authorities should delay dealing with it while deciding if doing so would impact on constitutional rights. Like all Americans, they want to be protected. Their idealism does not include a wish to die.

Many conservatives who support the administration are not unconcerned about people's rights. As recently as July

24, 2002, *The New York Times* reported that conservative leaders were worried that Attorney General Ashcroft was overstating the evidence of terrorist threats and feared that this was strengthening the kind of government power they oppose. "We need to ask ourselves," explained the president of the Family Research Council, Ken Connor, "how would our groups fare under these new rules?"[21] The White House has also sometimes taken steps to modify some of the hard-line recommendations made by Attorney General Ashcroft and other administration executives.

There can be no doubt that the September 11 attack, and the subsequent conflict with Iraq, involved the United States in a war against terrorism that heightened America's concern with homeland security. And it was—and is—inevitable that such a threat would cause those in charge of safeguarding the nation to press for security measures that conflict with the rights of individuals. It is just as inevitable that the issue of homeland security versus constitutional rights will continue to be debated as long as the crisis shall last. However, there is reassurance in the fact that time after time in our country's history, while liberties and rights have been curtailed in times of war, they have always been put firmly back in place with the return of peace. This, too, is the American way.

1798   President John Adams signs into law the Alien and Sedition Acts; twenty-five political opponents are jailed.

1861   President Abraham Lincoln suspends the writ of habeas corpus; 13,000 people are held without trial.

1942   August 8—Eight World War II saboteurs, tried secretly by a military tribunal, are convicted; six are executed.

1943   U.S. Supreme Court upholds President Roosevelt's Executive Order 9066 authorizing internment of Japanese Americans.

1964   Congress passes the Gulf of Tonkin Resolution giving the president authority to oppose aggression.

1970   Gulf of Tonkin Resolution is repealed by Congress.

1972   National Neighborhood Watch is founded.
       U.S. signs UN "Convention on the Prohibition of Biological Weapons."

1973   War Powers Act, which "prohibits the President from waging war beyond sixty days without Congressional approval" is passed by Congress.

1988   President Ronald Reagan apologizes to Japanese Americans for World War II internment.

1993   U.S. signs revised agreement spelling out inspection procedures for biological weapons.

1997   CIA begins a secret program to "create small bombs that could emit clouds of lethal germs."

2001 August 16—Zacarias Moussaoui, later charged with involvement in the September 11 attack, is arrested for an alleged passport violation.

September 11—Four airliners are hijacked. Two crash into the World Trade Center in New York City, destroying them. One crashes into the Pentagon in Washington, D. C. The fourth is forced to crash in Pennsylvania when passengers resist the hijackers.

September 18—Letters containing anthrax mailed to the *New York Post* and NBC news commentator Tom Brokaw.

September 24—President Bush signs executive order freezing all bin Laden and al Qaeda assets in the United States.

October—American Public Health Association (APHA) compiles "Guiding Principles for a Public Health Response to Terrorism"; Office of Strategic Influence (OSI) is established with no fanfare, and a multimillion dollar budget.

October 1—First anthrax death occurs in Florida.

October 7—U.S. planes strike terrorist camps in Afghanistan.

October 8—Office of Homeland Security established with Thomas J. Ridge as director.

October 9—Anthrax letter received by Senate Majority Leader Tom Daschle.

October 26—President Bush signs the USA PATRIOT Act into law.

October 29—Homeland Security Director Ridge issues the first security alert to the public.

November 13—The president declares an "extraordinary emergency" and signs the executive order authorizing secret military tribunals to try terrorists.

November 16—Anthrax letter addressed to Senator Patrick Leahy of Vermont is found.

December—American John Walker Lindh is found among Taliban prisoners.

December 26—Congress passes "Bioterrorism Preparedness Act of 2001."

2002 January—U.S. Defense Department releases photos of prisoners arriving at Guantánamo in shackles and blindfolded; foreign governments and human rights groups protest.

January 11—Justice Department releases information on 725 detainees they are holding.

February—*Time* magazine reports charges of lax security at U.S. Army Medical Research Institute of Infectious Diseases (USAM-

RIID); American Civil Liberties Union (ACLU), after repeated requests, is granted permission to interview detainees held in New Jersey jails; Bush administration announces Taliban prisoners, but not al Qaeda prisoners, will be treated according to the Geneva Conventions; in mid-month, existence of OSI is made public and within a week is closed down.

March—Civil liberties organizations conduct "Know Your Rights" sessions for New Jersey detainees; by mid-month, in the war against terrorism, U.S. troops are active in the Philippines, Yemen, and the Republic of Georgia.

March 6—$2 million added to federal funding of the Neighborhood Watch program to aid war against terrorism; National Crime Prevention Council releases Citizens' Preparedness Guide.

March 12– Color-coded terrorism alert system announced by Homeland Security Director.

March 28—Justice Department announces it will seek death penalty in Moussaoui case, denying protest by France not to do so.

April 3—Pictures of John Walker Lindh strapped naked to a stretcher and blindfolded are released amid charges of torture.

August—Terrorist Information and Prevention System (Operation TIPS) scheduled to begin in ten U.S. cities. .

June 6—President Bush announces he will ask Congress to create a cabinet-level Department of Homeland Security with control over twenty-two related agencies.

September—One year after the terrorist attack on the United States, more than 450 accused al Qaeda and Taliban fighters are still being held at Guantanamo.

October—Four Guantanamo prisoners are released without explanation and flown to Islamabad.

November 26—President Bush signs legislation creating the cabinet-level Department of Homeland Security with Tom Ridge at the head.

2003   March—Department of Homeland Security embarrassed when four armed Cubans land on Florida coast without being detected.

May—Bush administration announces it will release four underage Guantanamo prisoners in addition to twenty-two already released. Over four hundred are still being held.

May 12—Simulated terrorist attacks set up by Department of Homeland Security take place in Seattle and Chicago at a cost of $16 million.

Alien and Sedition Acts—laws passed under President John Adams making it a crime to speak or write critically of the president and authorizing him to imprison or deport aliens without trial

al Jazeera (The Island in Arabic)—leading Arab TV network in the Middle East with a viewing audience of 35 million people

al Qaeda—anti-American international terrorist group financed and run by Osama bin Laden

American-Arab Anti-Discrimination Committee—organization fighting discrimination against Arabs and Arab Americans in the United States

American Civil Liberties Union (ACLU)—leading watchdog organization concerned with violations of constitutional law and/or civil rights

American Public Health Association—independent group that compiled "Guiding Principles for a Public Health Response to Terrorism" differing from government recommendations

Amnesty International—organization concerned with violations of human rights in countries around the world

anthrax—deadly bacteria around which spores form and reproduce

Bill of Rights—first ten amendments to the Constitution of the United States

Bioterrorism Preparedness Act of 2001—measure appropriating $3 billion to fight bioterrorism in 2002

black campaigns—secret operations ranging from spreading disinformation to destabilizing unfriendly foreign governments

Border Patrol—U.S. immigration officers guarding our borders against entry by illegal aliens

Camp X-Ray—holding facility for enemies taken prisoner in Afghanistan

Centers for Disease Control and Prevention (CDC)—U.S. government agency charged with tracking the spread of disease and averting epidemics

Central Intelligence Agency (CIA)—clandestine government organization that deals with espionage and counterespionage in order to protect U.S. interests beyond the nation's borders

Citizen Corps—subdivision of USA Freedom Corps made up of Community Emergency Response Teams, Medical Reserve Corps, Neighborhood Watch, and Operation TIPS

Citizens' Preparedness Guide—twenty-eight-page document designed to help citizens deal with terrorism

Convention on the Prohibition of Biological Weapons—1972 UN agreement, revised in 1993, outlawing production of biological weapons and prescribing inspection procedures

Council on American-Islamic Relations (CAIR)—organization that monitors bias incidents against Islamic Americans and tries to improve relations with the community at large

cyber-terrorists—hackers who break computer codes in order to damage electronic systems necessary to the general health and safety

detainee—prisoner held without being charged with an offense

Executive Order 9066—President Franklin Roosevelt's decree authorizing the roundup and detention of Japanese Americans during World War II

Ex Parte Quirin—unanimous decision reached by the 1942 U.S. Supreme Court validating the creation of military tribunals

Family Educational Rights and Privacy Act—federal law preventing colleges and universities from releasing information about students without their permission

Federal Aviation Authority (FAA)—agency that regulates airlines and airports

Federal Bureau of Investigation (FBI)—agency responsible for fighting crime and terrorism within the borders of the United States

Federal Death Penalty Act—1994 law authorizing capital punishment for "conspiracy to commit acts of terrorism" and sixty other offenses

Flight Watch America, Inc.—outfit offering classes to teach passengers how to react in case of a terrorist attack aboard a plane

Foreign Intelligence Surveillance Act (FISA)—federal law authorizing secret panels of judges to hear evidence involving wiretaps and classified information

Foreign Terrorist Tracking Task Force—agency created by President Bush after September 11 attack and charged with detaining or deporting aliens suspected of supporting terrorists

Freedom of Information Act—federal law that government investigative agencies, such as the FBI and CIA, must reveal contents of files held on a person at his or her request

Geneva Conventions—set of international agreements for the protection of victims of war, including prisoners of war (POWs)

Guantánamo—military base leased to the United States on the island of Cuba

Gulf of Tonkin Resolution—passed by Congress after an alleged attack on U.S. ships in the Gulf of Tonkin, it empowered the president to take aggressive actions without consulting Congress

habeas corpus—order requiring a prisoner to be brought before a court to decide the legality of his or her imprisonment

Homeland Security Council—advisory group composed of various cabinet members, the heads of the CIA, FBI, and INS

Immigration and Naturalization Service (INS)—U.S. government agency responsible for tracking aliens and guarding the nation's borders

INS Detention Standards—rules ordering programs to inform detainees of their rights

"Know Your Rights"—jail program for detainees provided by a coalition of civil rights organizations

military tribunals—nonjury courts presided over by military officers, which are not subject to many of the rules of evidence governing civilian courts

mujahideen—Taliban soldiers originally armed and trained by the United States to fight Soviets

National Neighborhood Watch—volunteer program founded in 1972 to fight crime, which was funded with an additional $2 million to fight terrorism in March 2002

North American Aerospace Defense Command (NORAD)—air force authority responsible for the safety of the skies over the United States and in the immediate vicinity

Office of Homeland Security—U.S. agency established by executive order of the president following September 11 and charged with guarding against further terrorist attacks

Office of Strategic Influence (OSI)—former Pentagon agency whose duties included spreading disinformation

Orange Hat Patrols—Neighborhood Watch groups that wear distinctive orange headgear

Sikhs—Hindu religious sect, which rejects the caste system defining people's status by their birth

"sneak-and-peek"—denoting searches done without the knowledge or consent of the one being investigated

"Sunset Provision"—USA PATRIOT Act expiration clause ending its "enhanced surveillance" features in 2005 unless renewed by Congress

Taliban—fundamentalist Muslim group that formerly ruled Afghanistan, sheltered Osama bin Laden and al Qaeda, and terrorized the Afghan people

Terrorist Information and Prevention System (Operation TIPS)—program to enlist the civilian population in supplying information to prevent terrorism

USA Freedom Corps—government umbrella organization with an overall mission of preventing, or reacting to, terrorism

USA PATRIOT Act—federal law passed following the attack of September 11 that expanded the powers of the FBI, the CIA, and the Treasury Department to fight terrorism

War Powers Act—law prohibiting the president from waging war beyond sixty days without congressional approval

FOR MORE INFORMATION

Burgan, Michael, and Arthur Meier Schlesinger. *John Adams: Second U.S. President.* New York: Chelsea House Publishing, 2000.

Dudley, William, ed. *Japanese American Internment Camps: At Issue in History.* San Diego: Greenhaven Press, 2001.

Life Magazine Staff, ed. *One Nation: America Remembers September 11, 2001.* New York: Little Brown & Company, 2001.

McCourt, Frank. *Brotherhood.* New York: Sterling Publications, 2001

Neely, Mark E. Jr. *The Fate of Liberty: Abraham Lincoln and Civil Liberties.* New York: Oxford University Press, 1992.

Stewart, Gail. *America Under Attack: September 11, 2001.* San Diego: Lucent Books, 2002.

Zinn, Howard. *A People's History of the United States.* New York: Harper & Row, Publishers, 1980.

———. *Declarations of Independence.* New York: HarperCollins Publishers, 1990.

INTERNET SITES

American Civil Liberties Union (ACLU) Online Community Forum
forums.aclu.org/

Amnesty International USA
   www.amnestyusa.org
Council on American Islamic Relations (CAIR)
   www.cair-net.org/asp/article.asp?articleid=559&articletype=3
Geneva Convention Relative to the Treatment of Prisoners of War
   from the Office of the High Commissioner for Human Rights,
   adopted August 12, 1949.
   www.unhchr.ch/html/menu3/b/91.htm
United for a Stronger America: Citizens' Preparedness Drive, published by U.S. Department of Justice and National Crime
   Prevention Council, January 2002.
   www.google.com/search?q=cache:tIN77e.../cpg.pdf+Citizens
   +Preparedness+Guide&hl=e

SOURCE NOTES

CHAPTER 1

1. Author uncredited, "Minor Fame, Major Fun," from *The New York Times* on the Web. www.legacy.com/nytimes/Sept11.asp? Page=TributeStory&PersonID=147182

2. Author uncredited, September 11: "Chronology of Terror," from CNN, p. 1, www.cnn.com/2001/US/09/11/chronology. attack/

3. Kim Barker, Louise Kiernan, and Steve Mills, "The Heroes of Flight 93," from *The Seattle Times*, October 2, 2001. www.september11news.com/Flight93.htm

4. September 11: "Chronology of Terror," p. 3.

5. Jon Frandsen, "Bush Freezes bin Laden's Assets," from Gannett News Service and pressconnects.com.

6. Ian Christopher McCaleb, "Bush Announces Opening of Attacks," from CNN, p. 2, www.cnn.com/2001/US/10/07/ ret.attack. Bush/index.html.

CHAPTER 2

1. Evan Thomas and Michael Isikoff, "Justice Kept in the Dark," in *Newsweek*, December 10, 2001, p. 40.

2. David Johnston and Philip Shenon, "Man in Custody Since

August Is Accused in Terror Attacks," in *The New York Times,* December 12, 2001, p. B7.

3. Matthew Purdy, "Bush's New Rules to Fight Terror Transform the Legal Landscape," in *The New York Times,* November 25, 2001, p. A1.

4. Purdy, p. A1.

5. Jim McGee, "An Intelligence Giant in the Making: Anti-Terrorism Law Likely to Bring Domestic Apparatus of Unprecedented Scope," in *The Washington Post,* November 4, 2001, p. 2.

6. Purdy, p. A1.

7. George W. Bush, "Remarks on Signing the USA PATRIOT Act of 2001," from *Weekly Compilation of Presidential Documents,* vol. 37, issue 43, October 29, 2001.

8. Evan Gregory T. Nojeim, "Threats to Civil Liberties Post-September 11: Secrecy, Erosion of Privacy, Danger of Unchecked Government," from the ACLU, December 14, 2001. www.aclu.org/news/2001/n121401b.html; Michael Isikoff, "Justice Kept In the Dark," in *Newsweek,* December 10, 2001, p. 38.

9. Jim McGee, "An Intelligence Giant in the Making: Anti-Terrorism Law Likely to Bring Domestic Apparatus of Unprecedented Scope," in *The Washington Post,* November 4, 2001, p. A4.

10. Tim Weiner, "The C.I.A. Widens Its Domestic Reach," in *The New York Times Week in Review,* January 20, 2002, pp. 1, 7.

11. Evan Gregory T. Nojeim, "Threats to Civil Liberties Post-September 11: Secrecy, Erosion of Privacy, Danger of Unchecked Government" from the ACLU, December 14, 2001. www.aclu.org/news/2001/n121401b.html

12. Nojeim, December 14, 2001.

13. Sara Hebel. "Changes in Antiterrorism Bills Protect Student Records, College Lobbyists Say," in the *Chronicle of Higher Education,* October 26, 2001, p. A30.

14. John Burnett, *NPR Special Report: Strangers at the Gates.* www.npr.org/news/specials/immigration/immigration.html

15. Josh Meyer and Bob Drogin, "Response To Terror: Ridge Warns Nation to Remain Vigilant Through Holidays . . .," in the *Los Angeles Times,* December 4, 2001, p. A4.

16. George Lardner Jr. and Peter Slevin, "Military May Try Terrorism Cases; Bush Cites 'Emergency'," in *The Washington Post*, November 14, 2001, p. A1.

17. *Cato Daily Dispatch* for November 20, 2001. www.cato.org/dispatch/11-20-01d.html.

18. Thomas and Isikoff, p. 38.

19. *Times* editorial, December 7, 2001.

20. Author uncredited, "Last Night They Took My Husband Away!" from *Move-on*. www.moveon.org/constitution/

21. Author uncredited, "Last Night They Took My Husband Away!" from Move-on. www.moveon.org/constitution/

22. Author uncredited, "Muslim Secret Service Agent Removed" from Flight from Council on American Islamic Relations (CAIR), December 27, 2001. www.cair-net.org/asp/article. asp?articleid=559&articletype=3

23. Matthew Purdy, "Bush's New Rules to Fight Terror Transform the Legal Landscape," in *The New York Times*, November 25, 2001, p. A1.

CHAPTER 3

1. Naftali Bendavid, "Ashcroft: U.S. to Interview 3,000 More Arab Nationals" in *The Chicago Tribune* Internet Edition, March 22, 2002.

2. Tamar Lewin, "Cleared After Terror Sweep, Trying to Get His Life Back," in *The New York Times*, December 28, 2001, p. A.1.

3. Jodi Wilgoren, "Questioning With a Powder-Puff Edge," in *The New York Times*, December 13, 2001, p. B7.

4. Leslie Eaton, "Man Facing Perjury Charges Tells of Life in Detention," in *The New York Times*, February 19, 2002, p. A11.

5. Eaton, p. A11.

6. Editorial, "The War on Civil Liberties," in *The New York Times*, September 10, 2002, p. A24.

7. Author uncredited, "John Ashcroft Misses the Point," editorial in *The New York Times*, December 27, 2001, p. A30.

8. David Sarasohn, "Oregon Rains on Ashcroft," in *The Nation*, December 31, 2001, p. 7.

9. Author uncredited, "Police Nationwide Divided Over Whether to Cooperate With Federal Interviews of Middle

Eastern Men," from Associated Press (WABC Eyewitness News.) abclocal.go.com/wabc/news/WABC_12031_policein-terviews.html

10. "Police Nationwide Divided . . ."
11. Naftali Bendavid, "Ashcroft: U.S. to Interview 3,000 More Arab Nationals" in the Chicago Tribune Internet Edition, March 22, 2002.www.chicagotribun.../chi0203210186mar21. stort?coll=chi%2Dnewsnationworld%2Dhe
12. Philip Shenon, "Justice Department Wants to Query More Foreigners," in *The New York Times*, March 21, 2002, p. A19.
13. Sarasohn, p. 7.
14. Shenon, p. A19.
15. Bendavid.
16. Author uncredited, "USA: Post 11 September Detainees Deprived of Their Basic Rights," from Amnesty International Online, March 14, 2002. web.amnesty.org/ai.nsf/Index/ AMR510452002?OpenDocument&of=COUNTRIES\USA
17. Author uncredited, "Advocacy Groups Hold Rights Trainings for Jailed INS Detainees," from ACLU, March 13, 2002. www.aclu.org/news/2002/n031302b.html
18. "Advocacy Groups Hold Rights Trainings . . ."
19. David Johnston and Philip Shenon, "Man Held Since August Is Charged With a Role in Sept. 11 Terror Plot,"in *The New York Times*, December 12, 2001, pp. A1, B7.
20. Philip Shenon and Neil A. Lewis, "France Warns It Opposes Death Penalty in Terror Trial," in *The New York Times*, March 28, 2002, p. A14.
21. Larry Margasak, "U.S. Seeks Death Penalty for Moussaoui," from America Online (Associated Press), March 28, 2002.
22. Author uncredited, "Review & Outlook: Martyr-Piece Theater," in *The Wall Street Journal*, January 11, 2002, p. W11.
23. Karen Gullo, "Judge Denies Request to Televise Moussaoui Trial," from Associated Press (in the *Detroit News*), January 19, 2002. detnews.com/2002/nation/0201/20/nation-394846.htm
24. Margasak.
25. Sara Kugler, "Nation: Relatives Being Interviewed to Testify in Zacarias Moussaoui Case," from Associated Press (in *The Nando Times*). nandotimes.com/nation/story/322007p-2733257c.html

CHAPTER 4

1. Author uncredited, "CBS News Poll: The Home Front," January 27, 2002. www.cbsnews.com/now/story/0,1597, 325709-412,00.shtml
2. Dana Milbank, "In War, It's Power to the President," in *The Washington Post*, November 20, 2001, p. A01.
3. Author uncredited, "Alien and Sedition Acts," in the *Columbia Encyclopedia, Sixth Edition,* 2001. www.bartleby.com/65 /al/AlienNSe.html
4. "Alien and Sedition Acts."
5. William Miller, *A New History of the United States* (New York: George Braziller, Inc., 1958), p.140.
6. Miller, p. 140.
7. Miller, p. 142.
8. Jean L. McKechnie, ed. *Webster's New Universal Unabridged Dictionary, Deluxe Second Edition* (New York: Simon & Schuster, 1983), p. 815.
9. James M. McPherson, *Battle Cry of Freedom: The Civil War Era* (New York: Oxford University Press, 1988), p. 288.
10. *Encyclopaedia Britannica,* vol. 10 (Chicago: Encyclopaedia Britannica, Inc., 1984), p. 989.
11. McPherson, p. 289.
12. Author uncredited, "Supreme Court Weighs Civil Liberties During War," from the NYCLU. www.nyclu.org/wtc17.html
13. John Dean, "Military Tribunals: A Long And Mostly Honorable History," from *FindLaw's Legal Commentary.* writ.news.findlaw.com/dean/20011207.html
14. Tony Mauro (American Lawyer Media), "Historic High Court Ruling Is Troublesome Model for Modern Terror Trials." biz.yahoo.com/law/011117/73703-6.html
15. Mauro.
16. Declan McCullagh, "Why Liberty Suffers in Wartime," from *Wired News.* www.wired.com/news/politics/0,1283,47051,00.html
17. McCullagh.
18. Author uncredited, "Milnet: The War Powers Act of 1973." www.milnet.com/milnet/warpower.htm

CHAPTER 5

1. Mike Allen, "Bush Says Citizens Must Help in Fighting Terror;

President Cites 'New Responsibilities',” in *The Washington Post*, November 9, 2001, p. A1.

2. Tim Vanderpool, “A Vigilant nation, or Tattletale America?” in the *Christian Science Monitor*, January 23, 2002, p. 03.
3. Dan Eggen, “Neighborhood Watch Enlisted in Terror War; Citizens Urged to Step Up In $2 Million Expansion,” in *The Washington Post*, March 7, 2002, p. A01.
4. Eggen, p. A01.
5. Judy Keen, “Bush Promotes USA Freedom Corps in South,” January 31, 2002, p. A08.
6. Darragh Johnson and David A. Fahrenthold, “Front Lines on the Homeland Watch; After Ashcroft Plea, Neighborhood Patrols Pick Their Priorities,” March 8, 2002, p. B1.
7. Johnson and Fahrenthold, p. B1.
8. Johnson and Fahrenthold, p. B1.
9. Johnson and Fahrenthold, p. B1.
10. Mary Beth Sheridan, “Backlash Changes Form, Not Function; Sept. 11 Aftereffects Include Less-Visible Discrimination Cases,” in *The Washington Post*, March 4, 2002, p. B1.
11. Rachel Gordon, “Victims of Hate Crimes Recount Horror Stories/Outpouring of post-Sept. 11 Traumas in S.F.,” November 11, 2002, p. A.17.
12. Sheridan, p. B1.
13. Sheridan, p. B1.
14. Eggen, p. A1.
15. Author uncredited, “United for a Stronger America: Citizens' Preparedness Drive,” published by U.S. Department of Justice and National Crime Prevention Council., January, 2002, p. 24. www.google.com/search?q=cache:tIN77e.../cpg.pdf+Citizens +Preparedness+Guide&hl=e
16. Eggen, p. A01.
17. Eggen, p. A01.
18. Andrea Stone, “Ridge Announces New Terror Alert System,” in *USA Today*, March 13, 2002. www.usatoday.com/news/attack/2002/12/ridge-terror-alerts.htm
19. Stone.
20. Stone.

CHAPTER 6

1. Kate Randall, “Defending the Indefensible,” World Socialist Web

Site. www.wsws.org/articles/2002/feb2002/pows-f05.shtml
2. Leigh Sales, "Geneva Convention for Taliban Prisoners," Australian Broadcasting Corporation, February 8, 2002. www.abc.net.au/am/s476652.htm
3. Katharine Q. Seelye, "Rumsfeld Defends Treatment by U.S. of Cuba Detainees," in *The New York Times*, January 23, 2002, p. A9.
4. Seelye, p. A9.
5. Seelye, pp. 1, A9.
6. Seelye, pp. 1, A9.
7. Author uncredited, "U.S.: Geneva Conventions Apply to Guantánamo Detainees," from Human Rights Watch, January 11, 2002, Article 22. www.hrw.org/press/2002/01/us011102.htm
8. Carol Rosenberg, "Congressman Says Guantánamo 'Too Good' for Prisoners," in *The Daily Camera* (Knight Ridder Newspapers), January 26, 2002.www.thedailycamera.com/news/terror/jan02/26aguan.html
9. Author uncredited, "Congressional Report: Senator Inouye on Camp X-Ray," U.S. Department of State International Information Programs, February 1, 2002.
10. Martha K. Huggins, "Treat Prisoners Like Human Beings," in the *Albany Times Union*, March 26, 2002, p. A11.
11. Leon Wynter, "Interview: Robert Baer and Walter Pincus Discuss Forms of Torture," on National Public Radio Weekend Edition Saturday, February 9, 2002. New York Public Library, EBSCO.
12. Author uncredited, "Geneva Convention Relative to the Treatment of Prisoners of War," from the Office of the High Commissioner for Human Rights, adopted August 12, 1949, Article 17. www.unhchr.ch/html/menu3/b/91.htm
13. Wynter.
14. "Geneva Convention . . ." Article 5. usinfo.state.gov/topical/pol/terror/02020100.htm
15. Daniel McGrory, "Camp X-Ray Prisoners Urged to 'Come Clean'," from *The Times* (London), March 9, 2002, p. 18.
16. Stephen F. Hayes, "Let Them Starve," in *The Weekly Standard*, March 4, 2002. www.weeklystandard.com/Content/Public/Articles/000/000/000/979mnhen.asp
17. Author uncredited, "Al-Qaeda Suspects May Be Force-Fed," from the British Broadcasting Company News, March 31,

2002. news.bbc.co.uk/hi/english/world/americas/newsid_1903000/1903380.stm

18. "Al-Qaeda Suspects . . ."

19. Evan Thomas, "A Long Strange Trip to the Taliban," in *Newsweek,* December 17, 2001, p. 36.

20. John Riley, "Feds: Lindh Offered Regrets," in *Newsday,* March 30, 2002, p. A11.

21. Larry Margasak, "Lawyers Clash Over Lindh's Treatment," from Associated Press Online through EBSCO (New York Public Library), April 1, 2002.

22. Riley, p. A11.

23. Author uncredited, "'American Taliban' Torture Claim," from the British Broadcasting Company News, January 3, 2002. news.bbc.co.uk/hi/english/world/americas/newsid_1908000/1908618.stm

24. Katharine Q. Seelye, "American Charged as a Terrorist Makes First Appearance in Court," in *The New York Times,* January 25, 2002, p. A11.

25. Riley, p. A11.

26. " 'American Taliban' . . ."

27. Seelye, "American Charged . . .," p. A11.

28. "Convention (III) Relative to the Treatment of Prisoners of War."www.icrc.org/ihl.msf/7c4d08d9b.../6fef854a351b75ac 125641e004a9e68?

CHAPTER 7

1. Jeffrey Toobin, "Ashcroft's Ascent" in *The New Yorker,* April 15, 2002, p. 50.

2. Anthony Lewis, "Taking Our Liberties," in *The New York Times* Op-Ed, March 9, 2002, p. A15.

3. Author uncredited, "US Military Advisers Arrive in Georgia," BBC News, February 27, 2002.news.bbc.co.uk/1/hi/world/europe/1843909.htm

4. Patrick Martin, "US troops deployed to former Soviet republic of Georgia," from the World Socialist Web Site quoting *The Washington Post,* March 1, 2002. www.wsws.org/articles/2002/mar2002/geor-m01.shtml

5. Author uncredited, "Report: Hundreds of U.S. Troops Have

Arrived in Yemen," World Tribune.com, March 11, 2002. 216.26.163.62/2002/ss_yemen_03_10.html

6. Lewis, p. A15.

7. Lewis, p. A15.

8. Author uncredited, "US Threatens Iraq, Denies Specific Invasion Plans," from *Agence France-Presse*, May 5, 2002. www.spacedaily.com/news/iraq-02e.html

9. James Dao, "Congress Now Seeks Role on Measures Against Iraq," from *The International Herald Tribune*, July 18, 2002. www.iht.com/articles/64914.html

10. "President Delivers State of the Union Address," White House Press Release, January 29, 2002. www.whitehouse.gov/news/releases/2002/01/20020129-11.html

11. Author uncredited, "US expands 'axis of evil,'" BBC News, May 6, 2002. news.bbc.co.uk/1hi/world/americas/1971852.stm

12. Jonathan Weisman, "Pentagon Might Use Deceit in War on Terror," in *USA Today*, February 20, 2002, p. 4a.

13. James Dao and Eric Schmitt, "Pentagon Readies Efforts to Sway Sentiment Abroad," in *The New York Times*, February 19, 2002, from the Common Dreams News Center. www.commondreams.org/headlines02/0219-01.htm

14. Dao and Schmitt.

15. Damian Whitworth, "Pentagon 'Ready to Lie' to Win War on Terror," in *The Times* (London), February 20, 2002, Overseas News Section, p. 18

16. Dao and Schmitt.

17. Dao and Schmitt.

18. John Diamond, "New Pentagon Office Will Spread Disinformation to Throw Off Adversaries," in *The Chicago Tribune*, February 20, 2002. New York Public Library, EBSCO.

19. Author uncredited, "'Information' Office Closed," in the *Toronto Star*, February 27, 2002. New York Public Library, EBSCO.

20. Julian Borger and Patrick Barkham, "Attack on Afghanistan: Media: US Television to Censor Videos from Bin Laden: Networks Agree Limits on Tapes from Wanted Terrorist Leader," from *The Guardian*, October 12, 2001, pp. 1, 8.

21. Neal A. Lewis, "Ashcroft's Terrorism Policies Dismay Some Conservatives," in *The New York Times*, July 24, 2002, p. A1.

Ridge, Thomas J., 16, *17*, 18, 29, 75–77, *76*, 91
Roberts, Owen, 61
Roosevelt, Franklin, 56, 60–62
Rothschild, Peter, 71
Royall, Kenneth, 60
Rumsfeld, Donald, 78–80, 82, 91, 95, 100

Safire, William, 32
Saiya, Eddie, 10
Salaam, Joshua, 73
Salyer, J.C., 49
Saudi Arabia, 20, 21, 97
Security alerts, 29, 74–77, *76*
September 11, 2001, 8–10, *11*, 12, 50, 51, 53, 65, 88, 91
Serbia, 65
Service Employees International Union, 32
Sheikh, M. Siddique, 72
Solana, Javier, 80
Somalia, 21, 65
Soviet Union, 20
Spann, Mike, 87
Speziale, Jerry, 42
Sri Lanka, 85
Steckler, Craig, 44
Strossen, Nadine, 73
Student visas, 28–29, 37, 38
Sudan, 21
Sunset Provision, 25
Supreme Court of the United States, 59–62
Syria, 97

Taliban, 15, 16, 20–21, 78, 79, *81*, 86, 89, 90
Taney, Roger B., 57
Tanzania, U.S. embassy bombing in, 21
Terrorist Information and

Prevention System (Operation TIPS), 69–70
Thomas, Clarence, *17*
Torture, 84–85
Transportation Security Administration, 33
Treasury, U.S. Department of the, 24
Tregor, Jill, 71
Truman, Harry, 56, 64

United Airlines Flight 93, 10, 12
United Nations, 13, 96
USA Freedom Corps, 67, 69
USA PATRIOT Act of 2001 (H.R. 3162), 22, 24–28
U.S. embassy bombings (1998), 21
U.S. Postal Service, 70
U.S. Secret Service, 33–34
U.S.S. *Cole*, 94
U.S.S. *George Washington*, *14*

Vietnam War, 64–65

War Powers Act of 1973, 64
Washington, George, 59
Washington Post, The, 26
Weapons of mass destruction (WMD), 92, 96, 97
Wiretaps, 24, 26, 27
Worden, Simon, *98*, 98–99
World Trade Center, New York 1993 bombing of, 21, 23 2001 bombing of, 8–10, *11*, 12, 50, 51, 53, 88, 91
World War II, 60–62

Yemen, 20, 92, 94–95

al-Zaatari, Salam, 41–42